NAVIGATING TOUGH TEXTS *of the* OLD TESTAMENT

NAVIGATING TOUGH TEXTS *of the* OLD TESTAMENT

VOLUME 1

A GUIDE TO PROBLEM PASSAGES *from Genesis Through Deuteronomy*

TREMPER LONGMAN III

BakerBooks
a division of Baker Publishing Group
Grand Rapids, Michigan

Published by Baker Books
a division of Baker Publishing Group
Grand Rapids, Michigan
BakerBooks.com

Printed in the United States of America

Library of Congress Cataloging-in-Publication Data
Names: Longman, Tremper, III author
Title: Navigating tough texts of the Old Testament. Volume 1 : a guide to problem passages from Genesis through Deuteronomy / Tremper Longman III.
Description: Grand Rapids, Michigan : Baker Books, a division of Baker Publishing Group, [2026]
Identifiers: LCCN 2026008120 | ISBN 9781540971463 paperback | ISBN 9781493465422 ebook
Subjects: LCSH: Bible. Pentateuch—Criticism, interpretation, etc.
Classification: LCC BS1225.52 .L66 2026
LC record available at https://lccn.loc.gov/2026008120

Cover design by Sarah Gordon

Baker Publishing Group publications use paper produced from sustainable forestry practices and postconsumer waste whenever possible.

26 27 28 29 30 31 32 7 6 5 4 3 2 1

To my oldest grandchildren:
Gabrielle Gagnon Longman
Mia Katherine Longman

CONTENTS

ABBREVIATIONS

AD	*anno Domini* (in the year of the Lord)
ANET	*Ancient Near Eastern Texts Relating to the Old Testament.* Edited by James B. Pritchard. 3rd ed. Princeton University Press, 1969.
BC	before Christ
ca.	*circa*, about, approximately
cf.	*confer*, compare
chap(s).	chapter(s)
COS	*The Context of Scripture.* Edited by William W. Hallo and K. Lawson Younger. 4 vols. Brill, 1997–2018.
e.g.	*exempli gratia*, for example
ESV	English Standard Version
NAB	New American Bible
NETS	*A New English Translation of the Septuagint*. Edited by Albert Pietersma and Benjamin G. Wright. Oxford University Press, 2007.
NIV	New International Version
NJB	New Jerusalem Bible
NLT	New Living Translation
NRSVue	New Revised Standard Version Updated Edition

INTRODUCTION

Many Christians struggle with the Old Testament, and for obvious reasons. For twenty-first-century Christians the Old Testament is distant in terms of time, culture, and redemptive history.

In terms of time, the Old Testament is ancient, even more so than the New Testament. Though scholars dispute the dates of most Old Testament books, the biblical text itself would have us think that the oldest parts date to the time of Moses in the last quarter of the second millennium BC (Torah, Psalm 90). The most recent texts of the Old Testament come from the period after the Babylonian exile (post–539 BC; e.g., Chronicles, Ezra, Nehemiah, Esther, Haggai, Zechariah, Malachi), and some may be as late as 300 BC (e.g., Ecclesiastes). This means that these ancient writings come to us from well over two thousand years ago, and some reach back three thousand years.

In terms of culture, the Old Testament is from the ancient Near East. Every culture has distinctive ways of writing its stories and poems. Ancient Near Eastern narratives and poems are different from modern literature. The difference is not so great that the Old Testament is incomprehensible to us, but recognizing that it is from a different culture helps us understand why some stories and poems strike us as odd. As one example, in Genesis 20 Abraham complains to God that his household servant will be his heir because he has no son. The original reader would understand this based on contemporary custom, while the modern reader might be confused.

It should be obvious that there is a cultural distance between most twenty-first-century readers and ancient Near Eastern readers. Most people who read this book will read it in English. Of course, many people from all over the world can read English, including those from the modern Middle East. Sometimes people think that Middle Eastern readers (Israeli or Arab) have an advantage because they are closer to the Old Testament culture. But this assumption is incorrect. The culture of Israel today is significantly different from the culture of ancient Israel. It's important for all modern readers to acknowledge this difference; otherwise, we will read into the Bible our modern cultural understanding.

This cultural difference is why Old Testament scholars learn ancient Near Eastern languages, not only Hebrew but Ugaritic (the language of a Canaanite city-state), Akkadian (the language of the Babylonians and Assyrians), and Aramaic (the language of the people of Syria and eventually the lingua franca of the ancient Near Eastern world). Knowing these languages allows us to read the literature of the surrounding cultures and note similarities and differences compared to what we find in the Old Testament.

Finally, and perhaps most significantly, there is a redemptive-historical difference between the Old Testament and modern Christian readers. We live in the time after Jesus has come, and the Old Testament was written before that time. While there is continuity between the two testaments, there is also discontinuity, which can make the Old Testament difficult for us to understand. In this volume on the Torah, we will discuss, for example, topics such as sacrifices and divine warfare. We will ask questions such as why God's people could not eat certain foods or wear clothing made from two different types of fabrics.

These are reasons why Christians find the Old Testament tough, but some texts are more difficult than most. Passages that modern readers find especially difficult to understand are the subject of this book. This volume is on the Torah, also called the Pentateuch. The plan is to publish additional volumes that cover the rest of the Old Testament.

As we get into these texts, we need to remember that they are among the most difficult. They are difficult for a reason, and I intend to give the best explanations that I can. I have been professionally studying and teaching the Old Testament for over forty years. That does not mean these texts are simple to me or that I can give dogmatic answers to our questions about them. But they are not totally incomprehensible, and I will give as full and honest an interpretation as I can. Those who claim that they find these passages easy and give dogmatic interpretations are fooling themselves. Nonetheless, I believe you, the reader, will find this book helpful as you think through these texts.

That there are tough texts in the Bible troubles some Christian readers. Even some Bible teachers act as if there are clear answers to our interpretive questions. We need to remember that, though the Bible is without error, our interpretations of the Bible are not necessarily infallible, a statement particularly true of the texts we will be considering in this book.

Since our faith is based on what the Bible teaches, does interpretive uncertainty throw that faith into question? Not at all. To say that there are difficult texts does not mean that the interpretation of the Bible's fundamental teaching is up for grabs.

The Reformers were right to insist on what theologians call the perspicuity (a technical term for clarity) of Scripture. But these theologians did not believe that all of Scripture was equally clear. The seventeenth-century Reformed confession known as the Westminster Confession of Faith puts it extremely well:

> All things in Scripture are not alike plain in themselves, nor alike clear unto all; yet those things which are necessary to be known, believed, and observed, for salvation, are so clearly propounded,

> and opened in some place of Scripture or other, that not only the learned, but the unlearned, in a due use of the ordinary means, may attain unto a sufficient understanding of them. (1.7)

Those things in Scripture that are necessary for our salvation are perfectly clear. God created everything, including us. He created us innocent, but humanity has chosen to rebel against him, so we are sinners who need rescue. Jesus died on the cross and was raised in order to reconcile sinners to God. Jesus is coming again to put all things right and bring us to himself. Jesus is fully God and fully human. God is three in one, Father, Son, and Holy Spirit. These essential matters are clearly taught in Scripture. The essential teachings of Scripture are expressed in what might be considered the primary creeds of the church (Apostles' Creed, Nicene Creed, Athanasian Creed).

Other passages in Scripture are not as clear and often are a matter of debate among Christians. Since these are not essential for salvation, we can discuss and debate them but not treat them as issues that put people outside the Christian camp. The passages chosen for inclusion in this volume are the most difficult in the Torah. I give the best interpretation I can in the literary, historical, and cultural context in which they were written.

How to Use This Book

Eighty-seven chapters in this book deal with a single difficult text, but the chapter numbering goes up to 109 because some chapters address issues found in other passages in the Torah. For example, I treat a few of the Ten Commandments in the chapters on Deuteronomy 5, but if a reader turns to the commandments that are also found in Exodus 20, they will see a cross-reference to the chapters on Deuteronomy 5.

The title of each chapter is a quote from the passage itself, followed by citations of the verse containing the quote and the whole passage under consideration. Chapters with cross-references to other chapters also begin with a quote and citations of the verse and passage as a whole. These chapters then refer to the other chapter by number.

In this volume on the Pentateuch, each major section begins with a short introductory essay, followed by the individual chapters of that section. This provides a broader context for the individual passages that follow. Readers will get the most out of this book if, when they select individual chapters in a particular section, they begin by reading that section's introductory essay. The table of contents indicates the locations of these introductions.

I use the New Living Translation throughout with only a few noted exceptions. The NLT is clear and accurate, and in the spirit of full disclosure, I am one of the Senior Translators.

GENESIS 1-11

The Primeval History

Genesis 1–11 (technically Gen.1:1–11:26) is one of the most exciting, important, and challenging sections of the Old Testament. Even though it contains difficult texts, the overall message is clear and also foundational to the rest of the Bible. Genesis 1–2 proclaims that God created the cosmos and everything in it—including human beings. When he completed his work of creation, everything was very good, including human beings, who were created in the image of God, morally innocent, and living in harmony with God, each other, and creation.

Genesis 3 tells us why we don't experience the world as depicted in Genesis 1–2. Genesis 3 presents the story of the first human sin. That sin, committed by breaking God's command not to eat from the tree of the knowledge of good and evil, shattered the harmony of God's original creation. Sin provoked God's judgment, which included expulsion from the garden and the entrance of death into human experience. Relationships were broken (3:16), work became frustrating (3:17–19), and hostility emerged on both a human and spiritual level (3:14–15).

However, God did not give up on his human creatures. He judged their sin, but he also extended tokens of his grace. To Adam and Eve, he gave clothes to cover the nakedness that now brought them shame (Gen. 3:21). Themes of sin, judgment, and grace follow in the remaining chapters of this section of Scripture: Cain and Abel (4:1–16), the flood (Gen. 6–9), and the Tower of Babel (11:1–9). These stories are connected by genealogies that show the flow of time from the creation to the call of Abraham.

Genesis 1–11 is about the deep past, from creation to the time of Abraham. The genealogies give a sense of the passage of time, but they are not exhaustive and do not intend to give a timeline. They do not intend to inform the reader when the creation took place (see figurative language in chaps. 2, 3, and 5 below), so we can turn to evidence from the cosmos itself to explore that question. If the numerous lines of scientific evidence are to be trusted (and there is every reason to think they can be), then the creation happened around 13.8 billion years ago. If this is so, then the time between Genesis 1 and 11 is extraordinarily long. Thus the selectivity of the biblical account leaves us with questions we can't answer (e.g., What are the origins of the serpent of Gen. 3:1? How do the dinosaurs fit into the biblical account?).

The purpose of Genesis 1–11 is to provide a background for the call of Abraham in Genesis 12:1–3, and the purpose of the book of Genesis is to introduce the main story of the Torah, which is the exodus from Egypt. There are abundant signals that Genesis 1–11, like Genesis 12 and following, describes real history—namely what actually happened in the past. But there are also many signals that the history in these chapters is portrayed using figurative language. When it comes to the creation accounts in Genesis 1 and 2, the emphasis is on the proclamation that God, the God of Israel known as Yahweh, is the creator of all things and all creatures, including human beings.

Humans, while innocent at creation and in a harmonious relationship with God (Gen. 1–2), sin and shatter that harmony (Gen. 3). Rather than giving up on his human creatures, God relentlessly pursues reconciliation with them, judging them when they sin but also extending his grace to them. The focus in

Genesis 1–11 is on the whole world, and by the end of the section people still sin and reconciliation has not occurred. Genesis 1–11 provides the background, the reason why God will call Abraham and use him and his descendants to reach the world.

1. "The earth was formless and empty"

» Gen. 1:2; 1:1–2

The difficulty of the opening verses of Genesis is well illustrated by comparing Genesis 1:1–2 in the NLT, ESV, NIV, and NRSVue translations.

> In the beginning God created the heavens and the earth. The earth was formless and empty, and darkness covered the deep waters. And the Spirit of God was hovering over the surface of the waters. (NLT)

> In the beginning, God created the heavens and the earth. The earth was without form and void, and darkness was over the face of the deep. And the Spirit of God was hovering over the face of the waters. (ESV)

> In the beginning God created the heavens and the earth. Now the earth was formless and empty, darkness was over the surface of the deep, and the Spirit of God was hovering over the waters. (NIV)

> When God began to create the heavens and the earth, the earth was complete chaos, and darkness covered the face of the deep, while a wind from God swept over the face of the waters. (NRSVue).

Three of these translations (NLT, NIV, ESV) imply creation from nothing (*creatio ex nihilo*). The sequence is (1) no matter, (2) unorganized matter ("formless and empty"), to then (3) the organization of matter over the six days of creation. The NRSVue translation starts the story of God's creation with unorganized matter ("complete chaos") and then the organization of that chaos into the cosmos as we know it.

Both translations can be defended on the basis of the Hebrew, so the matter must be decided on other grounds. The first rendition (NLT, NIV, ESV) can appeal to later biblical texts, particularly in the New Testament, that make it clear that God created the cosmos from nothing (Rom. 4:17; Col. 1:16). God created everything, and there was no preexistent matter that God merely "shaped" into the cosmos.

The NRSVue translation (see also the NAB; NJB) can be justified by appeal to other ancient Near Eastern creation accounts (e.g., the Babylonian Enuma Elish and Atrahasis) that describe creation by the gods from matter that is just there.

The issue, however, is not as serious as many people think. The Bible clearly teaches that God created everything in the passages cited above as well as in Psalms 33:6–9 and 148:5–6 where creation from nothing is implied from God bringing things into being by his command. The question is whether Genesis 1 is concerned about that question. The ancient Near Eastern evidence suggests that ancient Israelites were not interested in the question of the origin of matter. That was an issue that concerned later thinkers (particularly in the Hellenistic and Roman worlds), so it is addressed in later biblical texts.

It's more likely that the NRSVue got the translation right since it conforms with the type of questions ancient Near Eastern people were asking at the time (i.e., not where matter came from, but how order came from disorder). Again, the overall biblical teaching is that God created everything from nothing, though this is not the focus of Genesis 1. The author of Genesis 1 may not have been interested in the origin of matter, but we can imagine that if he were asked who created the matter from which creation comes, he would say, "God, of course!"

There is another issue associated with these two verses. Based on a translation like that of the NLT, some believe that the fall of Satan happened in the gap between verses 1 and 2 (and thus this view is called the "gap theory").

The gap theory suggests that a lot happened in the "gap" between verses 1 and 2. In other words, when verse 1 says that "God created the heavens and the earth" it means he created it in its totality and completeness. Then when verse 2 says the "earth was formless and empty," it implies that something happened to turn the completed creation into chaos. What happened, according to this theory, is the rebellion of angels; Satan and his horde ruined creation so that God had to do it all over again. God had to take the now ruined creation and organize it once again into something orderly and habitable. That (re)organization takes place over the creation week described in Genesis 1:3–2:4a.

The reason for the gap theory arises from the following considerations. God created everything good, but from later Scripture we know there are spiritual beings known as Satan and demons. God did not create them evil, but we do not have canonical texts that fully explain their origin story. Therefore, people try to work the fall of some angels into the narrative, and they do so in the "gap" between Genesis 1:1 and Genesis 1:2.

This reading is unlikely. It is very speculative to read so much into a "gap." Also, it is at the end of the sixth day of creation that the author says everything is "very good" (Gen. 1:31), which means that there were no fallen spiritual beings present. The Bible does not answer all our questions, including when and why there are fallen angels (i.e., demons), so we should not try to force such an explanation into a gap in the biblical narrative.

2. "And evening passed and morning came, marking the first day"

» Gen. 1:5b; 1:3–31

Genesis 1 presents the creation as having taken place over a six-day period, followed by a day when God rested from his labors.

Each of the six days of creation concludes with the statement "and evening passed and morning came, marking the nth day" (1:5b, 8b, 13, 19, 23, 31b).

Does the biblical text intend for the reader to think that God created everything in six twenty-four-hour days? A surface reading of the passage might suggest this, but a closer look gives a different and more accurate impression.

Going back to the earliest days of the church, Christian theologians recognized that Genesis 1 intends to inform the reader that God created everything, but not how or when he did so. Augustine, writing around AD 400, said that the days of creation were not actual solar days (*Literal Meaning of Genesis* 5.5.12). To paraphrase Origen (ca. 185–253), "Who would be so foolish as to believe that the days of creation are literal days when there is not even sun, moon, and stars until the fourth day!" (*On First Principles* 4.1.16). Not being interested in describing how God did it, the Genesis author models God's creation using what the ancient audience would have understood as a regular work week.

The sequence of the creation days in Genesis 1 also suggests that the biblical author is giving a figurative description of God's creation. The following chart shows the parallel relationship between the first three days, which are realms, and the second three days, which are inhabitants of those realms. The sun, moon, and stars of day 4 fill the realm of light and darkness of day 1. The birds and fish of day 5 fill the realms of the sky and the sea of day 2, and the animals and humans created on day 6 fill the realm of the land created on day 3.

Day 1 Light and darkness	**Day 2** Sky and sea	**Day 3** Land
Day 4 Sun, moon, and stars	**Day 5** Birds and fish	**Day 6** Animals and humans

Thus, it seems unlikely that Genesis 1 intends to tell us how God created everything or how long he took to do so. But there is no doubt that the author challenges all other ancient creation accounts by proclaiming that it is Yahweh who was the Creator.

3. "So God created human beings in his own image"

» Gen. 1:27; 1:26–28

God created humans in his image. Without even knowing exactly what this means, we can understand that being made in God's image is a special privilege that bestows dignity on humanity. But the Bible never specifically defines what it means to be created in his image. This lack of explanation is almost certainly because the original audience knew exactly what was meant without further explanation. With a little study we too can better understand what the Bible means by "image of God."

Ancient Near Eastern kings sometimes set up images of themselves to represent their power and authority in their kingdoms. Thus, the book of Daniel uses the Aramaic equivalent of the word "image" (*tselem*) when describing how Nebuchadnezzar set up an image of himself on the plain of Dura (Dan. 3:1). Archaeologists of Tell Fekheriye in Syria have even discovered the statue of a king Hadad-yith'i that dates to the ninth century BC and has an inscription referring to the statue as the "likeness" and "image" of the king, again using Aramaic cognates to the Hebrew words used in Genesis 1.

In the same way that these statues, or images, represented kings in their kingdom, so human beings represent God in the world. They reflect the glory of God like the moon reflects the light of the sun. Being made in God's image confers great dignity on humanity; this is also communicated by the figurative depiction of the first human as from the dust of the earth (showing that humans are part of creation) but also from the breath of God (Gen. 2:7). This contrasts with Babylonian ideas that humans were created by their god Marduk from the clay of the earth and the blood of a demon god into which all the gods spit (see chap. 5 and the Babylonian creation myths Enuma Elish and Atrahasis).

We should also take careful note of the fact that God created both men and women in his image. Both reflect God's glory and authority in the world.

Understood in this way, the image of God is a status, not a particular attribute that separates humans from animals, as some theologians in the past have thought. The image does not reside in our reason or our language or some other characteristics that have been thought to differentiate humans from animals; rather, the image means human beings represent God in the world.

This status comes with a responsibility. "Then God blessed them and said, 'Be fruitful and multiply. Fill the earth and govern it. Reign over the fish in the sea, the birds in the sky, and all the animals that scurry along the ground'" (Gen. 1:28). As God's representatives in the world, the man and the woman are to expand their number by having children who themselves have children. They are also to subdue the earth and rule over the other creatures God has made. Some people understand these commands as permission to exploit and use creation for humanity's own self-serving purposes. A moment's reflection undermines that view. Humanity may enjoy a royal status in creation, but this status reflects God the king. And God is not a tyrant; he is a benevolent ruler who seeks the best for his subjects. Indeed, in this passage are the beginnings of a mandate for creation care, not abuse. Humans created in the image of God represent God the king in the world and thus are to be stewards of the rest of creation.

4. "Let us make human beings in our image, to be like us"

» Gen. 1:26

On the sixth day of creation, before God creates humankind, he proclaims, "Let us make human beings in our image" (Gen.

1:26). To whom does he refer when he says "us"? After the humans sin, when God ejects them from the garden, he announces, "Look, the human beings have become like us, knowing both good and evil" (3:22). Again, who exactly is included in the "us"?

Christian readers often too quickly read a reference to the Trinity in these verses. One can certainly understand why. We know there are three persons in the Godhead and all three were involved in creation. But we know about the Trinity from the New Testament (e.g., Matt. 28:18–20; John 1:1–3; 10:30; 2 Cor. 13:4; Col. 1:15–17), not the Old Testament. It is not until the New Testament that God reveals more about his trinitarian nature than we have in the Old Testament, which has at best glimpses of God's threefold nature. While God, a single being, has always existed as three persons—Father, Son, and Holy Spirit—he did not disclose his trinitarian nature until the New Testament. The book of Genesis was written to contemporary readers in a way that they could understand, and no one at that time would have thought the "us" was a reference by the Father to the Son and the Holy Spirit.

Some appeal to various grammatical explanations for the use of the first-person plural. Perhaps the most popular of these is what is sometimes called the royal "we." A king or a queen, even in modern England, might use "we" and "us" when they mean "I" or "me." A technical name for this use is the "plural of majesty." However, there is no evidence that kings, queens, or nobles of Israel or the ancient Near East referred to themselves using the plural of majesty.

The best explanation is found in the biblical conception of what has been called the divine assembly or divine council. This view does not hold that there are many gods, but rather that God is surrounded by heavenly beings whom he sometimes instructs and commands or with whom he confers, analogous to a king with his noble servants.

Consider the vision that the prophet Micaiah relates to King Ahab in 1 Kings 22. He sees God the king on his throne with "all the armies of heaven around him, on his right and on his left" (v. 19). These are angels who serve him. He then asks for a volunteer who will "entice" Ahab to attack the city of Ramoth-gilead, where he will be killed. One divine being/angel volunteers and accomplishes the task.

The opening of the book of Job is also instructive. After introducing Job, the scene shifts to heaven where "one day the members of the heavenly court came to present themselves before the LORD" (1:6). A number of other places in the Old Testament describe God as in the company of other divine beings (Isa. 6; Dan. 7:9–10), and special reference might be made to Psalm 82, which begins in the NIV, "God presides in the great assembly; he renders judgment among the 'gods' [*'elohim*, translated "heavenly beings" in the NLT]." The "gods" refers to the angels whom God criticizes for not taking care of the vulnerable.

5. "The LORD God formed the man from the dust of the ground"

» Gen. 2:7

The book of Genesis has two different accounts of creation. The first gives a cosmic perspective (Gen. 1:1–2:4a), and the second focuses on the creation of humanity (2:4b–25). Both inform the reader that God created everything, including humanity, but neither intends to tell us how he did it. Both accounts are figurative depictions of historical reality. Genesis 2:7 is a prime example of this. Ever since the early church, theologians have recognized that the description of God creating humanity from the dust of the ground and his breath does not intend to show the material means by which God made humanity. Rather it communicates that God created humanity and did so in a way that gives essential information about the nature of humanity and God's relationship with them.

After all, God is a spiritual being who does not have lungs. (Yes, God takes on human form in the incarnation, but for the Old Testament that is a future event.) The relevant question to ask is, What was the biblical author—including the ultimate author, God—trying to communicate in this figurative depiction of the creation of humanity?

The two components in this description, dust and God's breath, signify that humans are creatures just like animals but that they also have a special relationship with God. The picture of God breathing on the dust to form humans represents a form of intimacy and special relationship not shared by other creatures; it does not mean that the other creatures are not loved or of special concern to God. This figurative depiction of creation affirms what we learn in other ways in both Genesis 1 and 2. Humans are created in God's image (1:27, see chap. 3). In the first creation account, humans are God's final and climactic act of creation, after the rest of the creation has been prepared for their appearance on the sixth and final creative day.

Reading Genesis 2:7 in its original ancient Near Eastern context brings out another important aspect that this figurative depiction intends to communicate. The Babylonian creation accounts give a similar, though also tellingly different, description. In Enuma Elish, perhaps the best-known nonbiblical creation account, the god Ea, on Marduk's command, creates humans from the blood of a demon god. Atrahasis, a second Babylonian creation story, gives a fuller account:

> They slaughtered Aw-ilu, who had the inspiration
> in their assembly,
> Nintu mixed clay with his flesh and blood.
>
> That same god and man were thoroughly mixed
> in the clay.
> For the rest of time they would hear the drum
> From the flesh of the god the spirit remained.

> It would make the living know its sign,
> Lest he be allowed to be forgotten, the spirit remained.
> After she had mixed that clay,
> She summoned the Anunna, the great gods.
> The Igigi, the great gods, spat upon the clay.
> (*COS* 1.130:451, adapted)

In this passage, humans are formed from three elements. First, the clay parallels the dust of the biblical account. Both show that humans are creatures and "earthy." Second, there is a divine element. In the case of the Enuma Elish, the clay is mixed with the blood of the demon god Qingu. In Atrahasis, the divine element comes from a slaughtered deity named Aw-ilu, not specifically identified as evil. Still, at least in the Enuma Elish, the divine component indicates that humans were wicked from the start; this contrasts with the biblical creation account in which the breath of God confers dignity. Finally, in Atrahasis, the gods spit into the mixture, an act which then, as today, indicated contempt.

We should not read Genesis 2:7 to discover how humans were made, even though this figurative depiction clearly asserts that God created humanity. Instead, this verse tells us that humans are creatures like the other animals but they enjoy a special relationship with God. Rather than being evil, at creation humans both possessed great dignity and were morally innocent.

6. "In the middle of the garden he placed the tree of life and the tree of the knowledge of good and evil"

» Gen. 2:9; 2:8–9

While it is debated whether Eden is an actual place or a figurative depiction of a historical reality, there is no doubt that the tree of life and the tree of the knowledge of good and evil have symbolic meaning. How do these trees function in the story of creation and the fall?

First, let's consider the tree of the knowledge of good and evil. In Genesis 2, God tells Adam he may not eat the fruit of this tree, and if he does he is "sure to die" (2:17). But what does the tree stand for? The obvious answer is "the knowledge of good and evil," but in what sense? Adam (and eventually Eve) knows the difference between good and evil in an intellectual sense. Eating the fruit of the tree would violate God's command and therefore be wrong and thus evil.

But knowledge in the Old Testament often means something different than intellectual apprehension. To *know* something is often to *experience* it. A wooden translation of Genesis 4:1 is "Adam knew his wife Eve, and she became pregnant and gave birth to Cain." The noun "knowledge" in the name of the tree comes from the same root as the verb in Genesis 4:1, and clearly Adam did more than just become aware of Eve so that she became pregnant; he experienced her in the most intimate way. This is why most modern translations render "know" as the NLT does: "Adam had sexual relations with his wife, Eve, and she became pregnant."

By eating the fruit of the tree and so breaking God's command, Adam and Eve experienced evil. They did so by declaring their moral independence from God. In essence, they were proclaiming, "God can't define what is right and wrong; we will decide what is right for us." Of course, they were tragically wrong and the result was death, defined immediately by separation from a harmonious relationship with God, each other, and creation, but ultimately the result was physical death.

The tree of life is first mentioned in Genesis 2:9 as located in the middle of the garden of Eden along with the tree of the knowledge of good and evil. The symbolic significance of this tree is more immediately clear than with the tree of the knowledge of good and evil. It represents life—the life God has given to humans.

The next mention of the tree of life is in the aftermath of Adam and Eve's sin. Part of the punishment, and perhaps the most devastating part, that resulted from their sin was that God expelled them from Eden and separated them from the tree of life. Speaking to the divine assembly (see chap. 4), God says, "What if they reach out, take fruit from the tree of life, and eat it? Then they will live forever" (Gen. 3:22). Further, after their ejection, God placed cherubim and a flaming sword "to guard the way to the tree of life" (3:24). That is the last mention of the tree of life in the Old Testament, with the exception of its use in Proverbs as a metaphor for a long and happy life (3:18; 11:30; 13:12; 15:4).

But how does the tree of life function in the account of Genesis 2–3? Many people read Genesis 3:22 and 24 and think that the tree is magical in the sense that if Adam and Eve had eaten the fruit they would have lived forever, despite God's decision that they ultimately die. This understanding is very unlikely. We need to remember that God only told them not to eat from the tree of the knowledge of good and evil. While in the garden, they could eat from all the other trees, including the tree of life (2:16–17). By separating them from the tree of life, God introduces the process of death into the human experience.

While not mentioned again in the Old Testament, the tree of life reappears in the last chapter of the New Testament. Revelation 22:1–5 pictures the new heavens and earth as a restored Eden with the tree of life on each side of the river flowing from God's throne. In this way, John, the author of Revelation, communicates that the future involves a return to the beginning, but even better.

7. "The serpent was the shrewdest of all the wild animals the LORD God had made"

» Gen. 3:1; 3:1–24

The creation accounts of Genesis 1 and 2 give no hint of any problems in God's creation. In the first account, God finished his work on the sixth day, saw that everything he had made was "very good" (1:31), and rested on the seventh day. At the end of the second account, there is harmony between God and his human creatures, between the man and the woman ("now the man and his wife were both naked, but they felt no shame," 2:25), and throughout creation.

Thus, we are surprised when Genesis 3 opens with a serpent, "the shrewdest of all the wild animals," who starts questioning the woman in a way that raises doubt about God's competence and goodness. The serpent convinces the woman to break the command not to eat the fruit of the tree of the knowledge of good and evil, and the man quickly follows suit. The results are catastrophic. The relationship between the man and his wife is fractured, as is the relationship between them and God.

Who is the serpent and where did he come from?

Readers of the New Testament have a ready answer. The serpent is Satan. Revelation 12:9 identifies him: "This great dragon—the ancient serpent called the devil, or Satan, the one deceiving the whole world—was thrown down to the earth with all his angels."

While the identity of the serpent as Satan is clear from the New Testament, it is not likely that the original reader would have recognized this. We have to reckon with what theologians call progressive revelation. That is, God reveals more and more of his truth as we move through the Old Testament and into the New Testament. The former simply does not teach often or clearly about certain topics such as the afterlife, the trinitarian nature of God, or Satan. Yet, when the Old Testament is read in the light of the New Testament, we can see more clearly than the original audience could.

What would the original readers of Genesis, and likely any Old Testament reader, have understood about the serpent? First, remember that Genesis 1–11 talks about real events that happened in space and time but presents these historical events in figurative language.

The key to understanding comes when we realize that serpents, even walking serpents, appear in other ancient Near Eastern literature. They stand for evil powers that oppose the order of creation. Examples include the sea monster Tiamat, a serpent with legs whom Marduk defeats and then creates the cosmos from her body. In the Gilgamesh Epic a serpent steals the plant that might have given the hero eternal life. In the myth of Adapa is Ningishzida, a serpentine figure that guards one of the gates to the netherworld. Ancient Egypt also had serpentine figures that represented death and chaos, like the monster Apophis.

Thus, the original readers of Genesis would have immediately known that the serpent represented evil, even personified evil. The serpent's more developed identity as the devil comes in the New Testament. (Old Testament texts where the word *satan* appears—1 Chron. 21:1; Job 1–2; and Zech. 3:1–2—will be discussed in later volumes in this series.) Genesis 3 figuratively depicts historical reality; the author of Genesis wanted us to know that our ancestral forebears were seduced into sinning by an evil power, a personal one, who would be later known as Satan.

8. "It's only the fruit from the tree in the middle of the garden that we are not allowed to eat"

» Gen. 3:3; 3:1–7

See chapter 6.

9. "Look, the human beings have become like us"

» Gen. 3:22

See chapter 4.

10. "The Lord accepted Abel and his gift, but he did not accept Cain and his gift"

» Gen. 4:4b–5a; 4:2–5

Genesis 4 describes life after Adam and Eve have been ejected from the garden and start having children. Their firstborn was Cain, and the second was Abel. Abel was a shepherd, while Cain was a farmer. The narrator then reports that both men brought an offering to God. As appropriate to their occupations, Abel brings an offering from his flock and Cain brings produce from his fields. The narrator says that God "accepted Abel and his gift, but he did not accept Cain and his gift" (4:4). Modern readers often find this mystifying since no reason is given for why God liked Abel's sacrifice but not Cain's.

Some readers think the issue has to do with the fact that Abel brought an animal sacrifice and Cain did not. They reason that this is the case because later atonement sacrifices are bloody sacrifices that require the death of an animal in place of the sinner (see Lev. 1 [chap. 65]). The problem with this interpretation is that there is no indication that Abel offers an atonement sacrifice (or whole burnt offering), an *'olah* in Hebrew. The Hebrew word in the Cain and Abel story is *minhah*, which is translated "offering" but has the sense of a "gift." Later, Leviticus 2 describes a *minhah* offering that takes the form of a grain offering (see chap. 66). Here in Genesis, it is perfectly appropriate for Cain to bring a gift offering from the field and Abel to bring one from the flock.

So why does God have a problem with Cain's offering?

First, we must understand something about how ancient Hebrews told stories. Hebrew narrators are rarely explicit about what motivates a character, whether human or, in this case, divine. Rather, the narrator signals motivation in a more subtle way, requiring the reader to pay attention to details. In the case of Cain and Abel, these details include how the offerings are described.

The description of Abel's sacrifice suggests quite a contrast to Cain's. Abel's offering consisted of "the best portion of the firstborn lambs from his flock" (Gen. 4:4). In other words, he brought God the very best he had to offer. Cain, on the other hand, brought "some of his crops" (4:3). Cain brought the ordinary, not the best.

The quality of the offering reflects the heart of the offerer. Abel honored God, while Cain went through the motions. God knew this, so he did not look with favor on Cain's offering.

God's rejection of Cain's offering didn't prevent Cain from doing the right thing. God gave him the way forward after criticizing him for responding with anger: "You will be accepted if you do what is right. But if you refuse to do what is right, then watch out! Sin is crouching at the door, eager to control you. But you must subdue it and be its master" (Gen. 4:7). Rather than doing "what is right," Cain murders his brother out of envy and tries to cover it up.

God is not fooled, and he punishes Cain by exiling him farther away from Eden and making him a wanderer. Even in his punishment, God extends to Cain a token of grace (as he did with Adam and Eve in Gen. 3:21). He puts a mark on him to protect him from those who might want to harm him (4:15). While we do not know what the mark was, it shows that God still cared for Cain.

11. "Methuselah lived 969 years, and then he died"

» Gen. 5:27; 5:1–32

Even today, when we want to say someone is really old (a relative assessment), we might say, "He is as old as Methuselah." This is because Methuselah is the longest-living person among the really long-lived people in Genesis 5, extending from Adam and Eve's son Seth down to Noah. Indeed, the person who was youngest at the time of his death (with the exception of Enoch, who was taken up to heaven at 365 years) was Lamech, who died at 777 years old.

Did people really live this long in the period before the flood? The answer to this question centers on how the ancient author wanted us to read Genesis 5 (and indeed Gen. 1–11). Christians disagree on the answer. After all, we can't prove that people lived this long in the distant past or that they didn't.

As suggested in the introduction to this section and in some of the chapters above, Genesis 1–11 is history—that is, it talks about things that actually happened in the past—but it is a figurative depiction of that history. It's not myth or legend; it is history, but as a figurative representation of history it is not interested in giving an account of the past that one might capture on film (speaking anachronistically).

It is possible that the author of Genesis 5 used hyperbole to make a theological point. The historical reality behind these long lifespans may be that lifespans were longer early on, but they got shorter and shorter as time went on. Whether the ages are hyperbolic or not, this appears to be the point that the book of Genesis is making. Not directly connected to Genesis 5, God shortens the human lifespan to 120 years on the eve of the flood because of humanity's sinfulness (6:3). Those who were born after the flood, starting with Shem (600 years) and ending with Nahor (148 years), lived much shorter lives (even accounting for hyperbole), and each generation was progressively shorter. So the theological point concerns the corrosive effect of sin over time. Even after the flood, some people lived longer than 120 years, perhaps because 120 years is itself a symbolic number based on the biblical idea that a generation was forty years. Thus, 120 years would mean that a person on average lived long enough to see their grandchildren.

Scholars have long noted that the Sumerian King List speaks of extraordinarily long reigns of early Near Eastern kings, particularly those from before the flood. Some of the reigns last tens of thousands of years (the longest reign was that of En-men-lu-Anna who reigned 43,200 years). The biblical authors may have been aware of a tradition that ancient humans lived longer in earlier times and used that tradition for their own theological and political purposes. The Sumerian King List was interested in showing how kingship was an institution that was a gift of the gods. It also showed how later dynasties, particularly those that were then current, were related to previous dynasties. It also forwarded the idea that there was always one dominant city-state in lower Mesopotamia.

12. "Then one day he [Enoch] disappeared, because God took him"

» Gen. 5:24; 5:21–24

Among the long-lived preflood ancestors (see chap. 11), Enoch stands out. He is listed seventh of the ten generations that span from Adam to Noah. He was the son of Jared and the father of Methuselah, but he is best known as the only one about whom the narrator does not say "then he died." Instead, his account concludes, "Then one day he disappeared, because God took him" (Gen. 5:24).

What does it mean that God took him, and where did he take him?

First, note that Enoch was middle-aged when God took him. Being 365 years old seems like extreme old age (see comments in chap. 11), but the other people listed in Genesis 5 live much longer, many into their 900s. Thus, Enoch was middle-aged for his time, taken long before he might have died.

Being taken by God means that Enoch did not experience death like all the others. But why? Even though the narrator does not explicitly present this as the reason (Hebrew narrative often suggests rather than names motivations), he does twice say (showing emphasis) that Enoch walked "in close fellowship with God" (Gen. 5:22, 24). We should read this statement to mean that Enoch avoided death because of what must have been exceptional obedience to God.

But where did he go? While the text does not say, there is little doubt about his destination. He surely went to be with God, who was so pleased with him. There is only one other person whom God took in such a way—Elijah. In that case, the narrator specifies the destination, saying that "Elijah was carried by a whirlwind into heaven" (2 Kings 2:11). This adds to our understanding of Enoch's destination as well.

13. "In those days, and for some time after, giant Nephilites lived on the earth"

» Gen. 6:4; 6:1–4

The four verses that begin Genesis 6 attract a lot of attention. The story they tell is intriguing but very hard to understand. Unfortunately, this combination leads to all sorts of fanciful interpretations. With such a passage, we need to exercise restraint and caution. One way to do that is to recognize what is clear about the story and what is difficult to understand.

First the story. As the population increases, the "sons of God" marry the "beautiful women" (lit: "daughters of men"; Gen. 6:2). God responds with displeasure: "My Spirit will not put up with humans for such a long time, for they are only mortal flesh. In the future, their normal lifespan will be no more than 120 years" (6:3). Whoever the "daughters" and "sons" are, their union disturbs God to the point that he restricts the human lifespan.

But who are they and why does God get upset? First, let's state what is clear: Some kind of sexual transgression is happening here. Whoever they are, the "sons of God" should not be having intimate relations with the "daughters of men." That is really all we have to know to make sense of the story since its purpose is to illustrate the great wickedness that leads to the judgment of the flood (Gen. 6:5).

Can we say more? I believe so, though with proper caution. It is likely that the original audience knew the identity of the parties involved. Indeed, the best answer to the question of who they are comes from ancient literature—not as ancient as Genesis but from around the time of Jesus.

Let's start with the phrase "the sons of God." In the Old Testament, this expression often refers to spiritual beings we now call angels. In Job 1 and 2, for instance, the Hebrew tells us that the "sons of God" came into God's presence (see 1:6 ESV). The NLT translates this phrase as "members of the heavenly court," while the NRSVue says "heavenly beings" and the NIV "angels" (see also Pss. 29:1; 82:1; 89:5–10). If the "sons of God" in Genesis 6:2 are angels, the most natural way to understand "daughters of men" is as human women in the same way that "son of man" in the Old Testament always means "human being" (particularly throughout Ezekiel, beginning in 2:1, where it refers to the prophet himself). Thus, the best understanding is that Genesis 6:1–4 describes the unnatural intercourse between humans and angelic beings—in this case, we would say fallen angels (demons) with human women.

Some people object that such relationships are impossible due to the spiritual nature of angels, using Jesus's words in Luke 20:27–40 as support. Sadducees, who do not believe in the afterlife, try to corner Jesus by pointing to a woman who has had seven husbands. They ask which of the seven will be her husband in heaven. Jesus responds by saying none of them because there will be no marriage in heaven "and they will never die again." In this respect, he says, "they will be like angels" (Luke 20:36).

According to this view, because it is impossible for angels as spiritual beings to have sex or get married, it is impossible that the "sons of God" are angels in Genesis 6. Other suggestions are offered. Maybe the "sons of God" are descendants of Seth, namely the godly line (Gen. 5), and the "daughters of men" are descendants of Cain, the ungodly line (4:17–24). Maybe so. One can see why God would not want godly men to marry ungodly women. But then why would such a union produce the Nephilim? By all accounts, these were extraordinary people in that they were "the heroes and famous warriors of ancient times" (6:4), though their name, which in Hebrew means "fallen ones," suggests they were not good people. Also, and we will deal with this passage later in the book, it is likely that they were unusually tall people (Num. 13:33; see chap. 81).

Again, the best, but not certain, understanding of the "sons of God" is that they were fallen angels. What Jesus said in Luke 20 does not undercut this explanation. First, angels/demons can take on human form (Gen. 18–19; Mark 16:5), and so they could impregnate women. Second, all the evidence we have indicates that Jews around the time of Jesus interpreted this story in Genesis 6 as involving fallen angels (see 1 Enoch 6–16). Even the New Testament suggests that Genesis 6 involves angels (2 Pet. 2:4; Jude 6). Luke 20:34–38 does not apply to this argument because apparently fallen angels are not in Jesus's mind, since Matthew clarifies that he is referring to "angels in heaven" (Matt. 22:30).

14. "The waters of the flood came and covered the earth"

» Gen. 7:10; 6:5–8:22

In response to humanity's corruption and violence, God determines to bring judgment in the form of a flood that "will wipe this human race I have created from the face of the earth" (Gen. 6:7). But he was still not done with the humans he had made in his image, and he instructed Noah—"a righteous man, the only blameless person living on earth at the time," who "walked in close fellowship with God" (6:9)—to build an ark for his family and for pairs of animals (or seven pairs in the case of clean animals; 7:2).

But what was the extent of the flood? The description gives the impression that it covered the whole earth. God says, "I am about to cover the earth with a flood that will destroy every living thing that breathes. Everything on earth will die" (Gen. 6:17). When the flood comes, the waters covered the "highest mountains" (7:19). Indeed, the water rose more than twenty-two feet above the mountains (7:20), and the ark later settled on Mount Ararat, which itself is almost 17,000 feet high. The biblical description certainly sounds like a global flood.

But if there were a global flood there would be geological evidence of it, which does not exist according to the best science available. For this reason, many biblical scholars say that the text does not describe a global flood. They rightly point out that the Hebrew word that is often translated "earth" (*'erets*) can also mean "land" and thus point to a more local or regional flood. Nonetheless, the covering of the mountains strongly suggests that the picture is indeed of a global deluge.

Both the global and local flood interpretations are based on a faulty understanding of the account, not only of the flood but all of Genesis 1–11. We have above made the case for Genesis 1–11 being history that describes events using figurative language.

In this understanding, there indeed was a massive regional flood in the Near East. One might think of a flood at the end of the last Ice Age, when melting glaciers may have caused the waters of the Mediterranean to overflow what is today Turkey, turning a freshwater lake into a massive body of salt water today known as the Black Sea. Such a flood would have impressed itself on the minds of the survivors, who would have passed down the tradition from generation to generation.

Different people groups would have told the story of the flood. Interestingly, we have a flood account from Mesopotamia that shares many similarities with the biblical account (the eleventh tablet of the Gilgamesh Epic), but it also has significant differences of detail. For instance, the biblical account attributes the flood to Yahweh, not the Babylonian god Enlil. The Bible also identifies the cause of the flood as human sin rather than the noise that humans make, disturbing the sleep of the gods.

In other words, the Mesopotamian version tells the story in a way that conforms to its pagan beliefs. The biblical version tells the story that points to the true God. It figuratively depicts this historical event in order to impart an important theological message.

Genesis uses hyperbole (exaggeration to make a point) to tell the story of the flood. It takes a massive regional flood and describes it as a global flood. It describes a boat of massive scale, larger than any other wooden boat constructed even to today. Human sin is described hyperbolically, where "everything they thought or imagined was consistently and totally evil" (Gen. 6:5).

In response to the question of whether the flood was regional or global, the best answer is that it was a regional flood that Genesis describes hyperbolically as a global flood (since Gen. 1–11 describes historical events using figurative language). The original readers would have recognized this since they were familiar with this way of depicting primeval history.

15. "It is the sign of my covenant with you and with all the earth"

» Gen. 9:13; 9:1–17

After the flood, God makes a covenant with Noah and the rest of creation. God had an intimate relationship with Adam that some scholars today call a covenant, though the Bible never does. Covenant is a legal metaphor of the relationship between two parties. Elsewhere we will explain the connection biblical covenants have to ancient Near Eastern treaties between a great king and a servant people (e.g., a vassal treaty; see the introductory essay "The Book of Deuteronomy"), but "covenant" may not be the right term to describe the relationship between humans and God before the time of Noah. After the flood, though, God clearly makes a covenant, a renewed relationship with humans and all creatures through Noah, who is a kind of new or second Adam figure in the book of Genesis.

The relationship with Noah is the first one explicitly called a covenant in the Bible (Gen. 6:18; 9:9). Later covenants will follow with Abraham (12:1–3; 15:18; 17:2), the nation of Israel (Exod. 19–24), and David (2 Sam. 7). Each has unique emphases while also building on the previous covenants without replacing them.

The unique nature of the covenant with Noah is that it is with all of creation, while the later ones are with specific people or groups. The heart of the covenant with Noah is that, after the devastation of the flood, God promises that the entire creation will not be subject to destruction by flood again: "Never again will floodwaters kill all living creatures; never again will a flood destroy the earth" (Gen. 9:11).

Noah and his sons also had responsibilities to fulfill in the covenant, and these responsibilities sound like renewals of those given to Adam but with changes reflecting the postfall situation. They were to multiply and fill the earth (Gen. 9:1; cf. 1:28). They are responsible for all other creatures, but now these creatures will be afraid of humans and humans can use them for food (9:2–4; 1:28–30). There is also a reminder that humans are created in the image of God, but with Noah it comes in the context of the horror of murder and its consequences (9:5–6; 1:26–17).

After describing the covenant with God's commitment to preserve creation and with human responsibilities, Genesis 9 ends with God giving a sign of the covenant. The function of a sign is to remind the covenant parties of their responsibilities. Most biblical covenants have signs, and the sign of the covenant with Noah is the rainbow (Gen. 9:12–17). Signs of a covenant align with their nature; in this case, rainbows appear after a storm, and the covenant with Noah comes after the flood. The rainbow may have further significance given its Hebrew word, *qeshet*, meaning "bow" and more commonly used in the Old Testament for a weapon, a bow that shoots arrows. It may be that God has warred against violent humanity, and he now "hangs up his bow" and starts over with Noah and his sons. The rainbow is a reminder of God's grace and his continued pursuit of reconciliation with sinful humanity.

16. "And he became drunk and lay naked inside his tent"

» Gen. 9:21; 9:18–28

After the flood waters subside, Noah and his family disembark. God enters into a covenant with Noah (Gen. 9:1–7), which re-establishes his relationship with humanity after the rupture of human sin and God's judgment (see chap. 15). What follows is to many modern readers an odd story.

The story concerns Noah and his three sons: Shem, Ham, and Japheth. The narrator mentions that Ham has a son named Canaan. What may seem like a throwaway line about Canaan is very important to this story and why it is told.

Noah plants a vineyard, drinks some wine, gets drunk, strips, and passes out in his tent. One might think that the narrator will focus on Noah's sin, but that's not what happens. Instead Ham, said for a second time to be the father of Canaan, sees his father naked in the tent and tells his brothers about it. This seems innocent enough, but notice what the brothers do. They don't look at their father but walk in backward and cover him up. When Noah sobers up, he curses not Ham but Ham's son Canaan. Then he praises Shem and Japheth, who treated him with dignity.

What is going on? What did Ham do wrong? Some people think the text is euphemistically suggesting that Ham had sex with his vulnerable father. This is unlikely, and if it had happened the narrator would have no problem stating it very directly. Ham's transgression is that he did not honor his father. In the ancient Near East, a son is to take care of his father when he is in a weakened or helpless situation. An interesting text describes the duties of a good son toward his father, "to take his hand when he is drunk, to bear him up when he is full of wine" (*COS* 1:344, adapted).

But why does Canaan get punished for Ham's transgression? We can't say for sure, but perhaps since a son (Ham) sinned against his father (Noah), a son (Canaan) suffers the father's punishment (Ham). We don't know anything about the person Canaan, but we certainly know about his descendants, the Canaanites. The Canaanites are the inhabitants of the land promised to Abraham, whom the Israelites later conquer and displace. Why? God anticipates the situation in Canaan when he tells Abraham that his descendants will take the Canaanites' land when "the sins of the Amorites [another name for Canaanites] . . . warrant their destruction" (Gen. 15:16; see chap. 21).

Before leaving this text, it is important to debunk an egregious racist interpretation of it. Interpreters have used this text to justify the mistreatment and even the slavery of Black people on the basis of the "curse of Ham." First, it is questionable to equate Ham's descendants with Black people, but even more to the point there is no "curse of Ham." It is a curse on Canaan (for more detail, see Longman, *The Bible and the Ballot*, 287–88).

17. "Let's build a great city for ourselves with a tower that reaches into the sky"

» Gen. 11:4; 11:1–9

As noted in the introduction to Genesis 1–11, the accounts after the Genesis 3 story of the fall (Cain and Abel in 4:1–16; the flood in Gen. 6–9) follow the same pattern. They recount human sin, followed by God's pronouncement of judgment, then a token of grace, followed by the execution of God's judgment. The Tower of Babel is the final story in this series and follows the pattern with one notable twist.

The story begins with a migratory group of people settling and deciding to build a city and a tower. The sin is gathering together to build a city and a tower. God had dispersed humans as part of his earlier punishments, causing them to wander (Gen. 3:23–24; 4:12), but here they gather together. They build a tower that "reaches into the sky" with the intention of making a name for themselves (11:4). Rather than calling on God and honoring his name, they want to ascend to heaven and make a name for themselves. Here we see a parallel with Adam and Eve who ate the forbidden fruit so they would "be like God" (3:5). Humans are made in God's image, but they are not God. To aspire to be God involves tremendous pride.

God then announces his judgment on humans to his angelic council ("let's go down," Gen. 11:7; see chap. 4). Up to this point in the story, there has only been one language, but God determines to "confuse the people with different languages. Then they won't be able to understand each other" (11:7). The narrator then immediately reports the execution of the judgment, which leads to the new name for the location—Babel. The name bears a resemblance to, though is not derived from, the verb *balal*, "confused."

But notice what is missing: the token of grace. Or is it? We might see grace related to this story in two ways. First, the judgment results in scattering and multiplication of languages, making human communication much more difficult but still possible. God does not completely remove humans' ability to communicate with each other. Interestingly, the previous chapter, Genesis 10, gives a kind of language map with different people groups and their languages. By not completely removing the possibility of communication, God provides an element of grace. The story also shows that bad things can happen when a bunch of sinners get together, so there may also be grace in scattering them again.

But why isn't the language map of Genesis 10 placed after the story of the confusion of the languages in the tower story of Genesis 11? Since the different languages result from the tower story, that would be expected. However, by moving the map before the tower, the narrator positions the call of Abraham as the next story (Gen. 12:1–3). In God's call for Abraham to go to the land he will show him and in the promises God gives him, a whole new chapter of God's grace opens for humanity. That is, the call of Abraham is the token of grace that follows the sin and judgment of the tower story.

Before we leave this story, we make a final comment about the tower. What does the text invite us to picture? If we read it as we should, in its ancient Near Eastern context, the tower is a ziggurat, the Babylonian version of a pyramid. It is a stepped pyramid, with its top thought to be a sanctuary in the heavens. The ziggurat in the ancient city of Babylon (the Akkadian name being not "confusion" but rather *bab-ili*, "the gate of the gods") was called *Etemenanki* ("the house of the foundation of heaven and earth").

GENESIS 12-36

The Story of the Ancestors

The primeval history is the backstory to the call of the first patriarch (or ancestor), Abram, whose name is later changed to Abraham. Genesis 1–11 has introduced God as the creator of all things, including humanity. Genesis 2 makes clear that at their creation humanity was morally innocent. Genesis 3 shows that evil is the result of rebellion and is not the creation of God. As we have seen earlier (see introductory essay for Gen. 1–11), Genesis 3–11 gives four accounts of human evil, God's determination to judge that evil, and also his continuing gracious desire and pursuit of reconciliation with his human creatures (the fall in Gen. 3; Cain and Abel in Gen. 4; the flood in Gen. 6–9; the Tower of Babel in 11:1–9).

The call of Abram (hereafter Abraham; see chap. 24) unveils God's plan for reconciliation. He would create a people who would reach the world to achieve that reconciliation. God calls Abraham to "leave your native country, your relatives, and your father's family, and go to the land that I will show you." If Abraham obeys, then God makes several promises: "I will make you into a great nation. I will bless you and make you famous, and you will be a blessing to others. I will bless those who bless you and curse those who treat you with contempt. All the families on earth will be blessed through you" (Gen. 12:1–3).

Though the word "covenant" is not used until later in the Abraham story (Gen. 15:18; 17:2), God enters into covenant with the patriarch at this moment. In Genesis 15 and 17 he reaffirms his commitment to Abraham. This covenant entails human responsibility (Abraham must obey the commands to "leave" and "go") as well as gracious divine promises. The promise of a great nation, a concern of the following chapters, requires many descendants (22:17) as well as land (15:17–20). Also, and very importantly, God promises blessing to Abraham and his descendants and then to all the peoples of the earth through them. Blessing here means having a harmonious relationship with God, which results in a harmonious relationship with other people and with the creation itself. As the New Testament will make clear, this blessing ultimately comes through Jesus, the true seed of Abraham (Gal. 3:16).

The fulfillment of these promises is in the future. Abraham has to live by faith, and the rest of the story concerns how the patriarch responds to threats and obstacles to their fulfillment. Does he respond with faith or doubt? The main focus of Abraham's faith journey is on the birth of a son. After all, how can he have many descendants if he has no son? Abraham's responses are shaky at best, with God reassuring him at key moments that he indeed will give Abraham a son (see chaps. 20 and 25 below).

God does give Abraham and Sarah a son in their old age, bringing to fruition the first step to fulfilling the promise that Abraham's descendants will become a great nation. The reader might think this birth marks the end of the Abraham story, but there is one more test for Abraham (Gen. 22; see chap. 28 below).

Eventually the narrative moves on to the next generation, to Isaac, who is heir to the promise and the one to carry God's purposes forward. Of the three patriarchs (Abraham, Isaac, Jacob), Isaac plays the most minor role. He is often described as the son of Abraham or the father of Jacob, and soon the narrative moves to the complex figure of Jacob. He is a deceiver and very self-protective. He also shows favoritism within his family by favoring his wife Rachel over his wife Leah, and his sons Joseph and Benjamin over his other ten sons. Still, God uses him to carry forward the covenant promises into the next generation. After an encounter with God, Jacob has his name changed to Israel (see chap. 33). He has twelve sons, all of whom are father figures for the future tribes of Israel. What we read in the book of Genesis about the patriarchs has implications for the future of God's chosen people.

18. "Tell them you are my sister"

» Gen. 12:13; 12:10–20

Abram (hereafter Abraham; see chap. 24) obeyed God's command to go to the land that he would show him, a land we later learn is the land of Canaan. If Abraham did so, God promised he would make him into a great nation, bless him and his descendants, and through them bless "all the families on earth" (Gen. 12:1–3). The promise of a great nation presumes land and many descendants. The story of Abraham (Gen. 12–24) follows his journey of faith. When obstacles threaten the fulfillment of God's promises, does Abraham respond with faith or with doubt? Does he trust God to fulfill the promises, or does he try to protect himself and manufacture the desired results?

The first threat comes in the form of a famine. When the promised land cannot sustain life, how does Abraham respond? Not well. He takes Sarai (hereafter Sarah; see chap. 24) to Egypt where there is food. But he does not trust God to keep him safe. He believes that if the Egyptians know he is Sarah's husband, they will kill him to get to her. He tells Sarah to lie about her relationship with him, saying she is his sister and not his wife. While she is Abraham's half sister (Gen. 20:2), telling her not to say she is his wife withholds the most important part of their relationship. Abraham lies to save his own life.

When they come to Egypt, the pharaoh notices the beautiful Sarah and brings her into the palace, while he gives riches to Abraham. Abraham's lie puts not only Sarah but the promise at great risk. If she became pregnant by Pharaoh, what would that mean about the promise of an heir? God graciously intervenes by bringing diseases on Pharaoh and his household. While this might seem unfair to Pharaoh, God's intervention prevents Pharaoh from continuing his relationship with Sarah. Somehow Pharaoh learns she is Abraham's wife and, after confronting Abraham, sends him away with Sarah "and all his possessions" (Gen 12:20).

God shows grace to Abraham even though his lie to protect himself demonstrates a lack of faith in God's promises. God not only brings him up out of Egypt unharmed but also richer. God has plans for Abraham, even though Abraham needs to grow in his faith.

While these events date to before the exodus from Egypt, the account itself was composed later and shares the same basic outline as the account of the exodus. Abraham was in Egypt because of a famine; the family of Jacob emigrated to Egypt because of famine (Gen. 46). God sent plagues on the pharaoh who took Sarah, leading to Abraham and Sarah's expulsion from the land; God sent plagues on the pharaoh of Exodus that resulted in Israel's departure from Egypt (Exod. 7–12). Both Abraham and the later Israelites leave Egypt richer than they arrived there (Exod. 12:35–36). The difference lies in the dubious behavior of Abraham, but both stories show how God uses his chosen people to reach the world.

19. "And Melchizedek, the king of Salem and a priest of God Most High, brought Abram some bread and wine"

» Gen. 14:18; 14:18–24

Genesis 14 tells the story of a raid into Canaan by four Near Eastern kings—the kings of Babylonia, Ellasar, Elam, and Goiim. At the time, Canaan was composed of city-states, each headed by its own king. Genesis 14 specifically names four of these kings: the kings of Sodom, Gomorrah, Zeboiim, and Bela. Elam's king Kedorlaomer had ruled these Canaanite kings for twelve years, but then they rebelled against him. The raid by the Near Eastern kings was apparently in reprisal for the Canaanites' rebellion against Kedorlaomer. They attacked and plundered several people groups and cities in Canaan, including Sodom and Gomorrah. They not only took the spoils of these two cities but also kidnapped Lot, Abraham's nephew, who was living in Sodom at the time.

When Abraham heard about the attack and Lot's capture, he mustered 318 men and set off in pursuit. He caught up with them in the north and recovered the plunder as well as the captives, including Lot.

As Abraham returned, the appreciative king of Sodom came out to greet him. The king offered Abraham the plunder, but he refused, most likely aware that the city was the epitome of godlessness (see Gen. 19). However, he expressed a completely different attitude toward a man named Melchizedek, a rather mysterious figure.

Melchizedek is king of Salem, almost certainly a reference to the city later known as Jerusalem. His name means "king of righteousness," and he was a king as well as "a priest of God Most High" (Gen. 14:18). As priest, Melchizedek blessed Abraham:

> Blessed be Abram by God Most High,
>   Creator of heaven and earth.
> And blessed be God Most High,
>   who has defeated your enemies for you. (14:20)

What is intriguing is that Abraham recognizes this king-priest as a fellow worshiper of the same God. Therefore, Abraham gives Melchizedek a tenth of everything.

Who is Melchizedek? Much of his identity remains a mystery. He is a foreign king, but he worships the right and true God. In this, he is similar to Moses's future father-in-law, Jethro, who is also identified as a non-Hebrew priest of the true God.

The book of Hebrews uses this enigmatic figure to talk about Jesus (Heb. 4:14–5:10; 7:1–28). Melchizedek is not a preincarnate appearance of Jesus, but he does become a template that the author of Hebrews uses to make the point that, unlike Israelite priests, Jesus is both king and priest. Hebrews also remembers that Abraham offered a tithe to Melchizedek. Since Abraham was the great-grandfather of Levi, head of the future priestly tribe and ancestor of Aaron, the first high priest, this gift showed that Melchizedek's authority was even greater than that of Levi. Associating Jesus with this priest-king showed that Jesus was vastly superior to Levi.

20. "You have given me no descendants of my own, so one of my own servants will be my heir"

» Gen. 15:3; 15:1–20

God appears to Abraham in a vision at a time when he doubts God's intention to fulfill the promise that his descendants will become a great nation (Gen. 12:2) because he doesn't even have an heir.

God's first words are reassuring. God tells him not to be afraid and that he himself is Abraham's protection and reward. Abraham's response mystifies modern audiences: "What good are all your blessings when I don't even have a son? Since you have given me no children, Eliezer of Damascus, a servant in my household, will inherit all my wealth" (Gen. 15:2). Why does Abraham talk about his household servant in this way?

Ancient documents from a Mesopotamian site called Nuzi (ca. 1475–1350 BC) help us understand what is behind Abraham's reference to Eliezer. In a day before retirement centers, the responsibility of caring for an aging parent belonged to a child; this is one of many reasons why not having a child, especially a son, was so worrying. In such cases, the childless couple would adopt a household servant who would care for them in their old age, and in return that servant would inherit the couple's personal property.

But this was not God's intention for Abraham, and he reaffirms his commitment that Abraham and Sarah will have a son of their own who will be their heir (Gen. 15:4). God then gives instructions to Abraham to perform a ritual that is also unfamiliar to modern readers.

God tells him to get various animals ("a three-year-old heifer, a three-year-old female goat, a three-year-old ram, a turtledove, and a young pigeon," Gen. 15:9). With the exception of the birds, Abraham was to cut them in half and place the halves opposite of each other. When the sun set, he suddenly "saw a smoking firepot and a flaming torch pass between the halves of the carcasses" (v. 17) as God reaffirmed his promises that Abraham's descendants would indeed become a great nation.

Ancient Near Eastern custom explains the significance of this ritual. When two people made a solemn vow, they would divide animals and then walk through the path between the halves. By doing so, each person took on a self-curse, in essence saying, "If I break my promise, may I be killed like these animals." Significantly, in the case of Genesis 15, only the smoking firepot and the flaming torch go through the halves, not Abraham. The firepot and torch represent God, who often appears as fire and smoke (e.g., the burning bush, the top of Mount Sinai, the pillar of fire that guided Israel in the wilderness). God alone takes on the burden of the curse to emphasize the fact that he will not break his promise to Abraham.

21. "For the sins of the Amorites do not yet warrant their destruction"

» Gen. 15:16

Genesis 15 recounts God's reassurance to Abraham that he will have a son and God will make him into a great nation (see chap. 20). But this promise involved more than just future descendants; it also included the promise of land. The assumption from the start was that this land would be "the land that I will show you" (Gen. 12:1)—namely, the land of Canaan.

Abraham traveled with his wife Sarah and his nephew Lot to that land, but during his life he wandered from place to place. It was not his land then, and even at the end of his life he only owned a small parcel that he bought to bury Sarah (Gen. 23:1–20). Abraham not only had to believe God that he would have many descendants but also that his descendants would possess the land in the future.

For this reason, in Genesis 15 God reassures Abraham about future possession of the land as well as descendants. This promise would not come to fruition for a long time. God informs Abraham that his descendants will be enslaved for four hundred years in another country, but "after four generations your descendants will return here, for the sins of the Amorites do not yet warrant their destruction" (15:16).

In this context "Amorites" refers to Canaanites. Later God will identify the extent of the future land ("from the border of Egypt to the great Euphrates River," Gen. 15:18) and the different ethnic or tribal components living in the land who will be displaced ("the land now occupied by the Kenites, Kenizzites, Kadmonites, Hittites, Perizzites, Rephaites, Amorites, Canaanites, Girgashites, and Jebusites," 15:19–21).

Very significant for our understanding of the later conquest is the reason for the delay of possession: "The sins of the Amorites do not yet warrant their destruction" (Gen. 15:16). The conquest was a matter of God's judgment on these people; it was not simply about making room for the Israelites to dwell in the land. When we reflect on Israel's wars on the inhabitants of the land (see chaps. 90 and 98), we will look back on this passage for the ethical and theological justification for the conquest.

22. "Go and sleep with my servant. Perhaps I can have children through her."

» Gen. 16:2; 16:1–16

In Genesis 15 (see chap. 20 above), Abraham's faith wavered as he and Sarah grew older and still did not have a child. How could God fulfill his promise that Abraham's descendants would become a great nation (12:2) if they didn't have that first child, a son to carry on Abraham's line?

At the end of Genesis 15, a reader might think Abraham was solid in his confidence that God would fulfill his promises. However, the very next story undermines this idea. Genesis 16 recounts an episode of Abraham's faith journey that begins with a suggestion by Sarah. She tells Abraham that since "the Lord has prevented me from having children," Abraham should sleep with Sarah's slave with the hope that *she* would have a child, and thus Sarah could "have children through her" (16:2). Notice that Sarah blames the Lord for her plight. For reasons we will explore in chapter 28, she is correct that God has kept her from conceiving. However, God has his reasons, while Sarah simply thinks he is either unable or unwilling to let her have children. She should have a confident hope, but rather she doubts.

That Abraham readily agrees with her plan shows that, in spite of his previous encounter with God (Gen. 15), his faith again falters. He sleeps with Hagar, described as an "Egyptian servant" (16:1), whom they most likely acquired while they were in Egypt being enriched by Pharaoh (12:16).

Hagar does become pregnant and begins to despise Sarah, who then, with Abraham's permission, mistreats her such that Hagar flees. God intervenes, telling Hagar to return and submit to Sarah. He promises that her child will have many descendants, "more descendants than you can count" (Gen. 16:10). Hagar does return to Abraham and Sarah and gives birth to a boy, whom they name Ishmael.

Genesis and beyond will show that Abraham and Sarah's plan to have a son through Hagar complicates matters horribly. Not only will there be conflict within Abraham's family, but there will also be conflict between the descendants of Abraham through Ishmael and through his future son Isaac, a conflict that many see continuing today between Jewish and Arab peoples.

It should not surprise us that Abraham and Sarah's strategy to produce a family with a secondary wife made things more difficult. They acted out of fear and a lack of faith that God would allow Sarah to get pregnant and have a child. As in Genesis 15 (see chap. 20 above), their actions to produce an heir reflect an ancient Near Eastern custom. Two examples that illustrate this custom will suffice. First, a tablet from Nuzi (a site near Abraham's homeland of Paddan-Aram from the mid-second millennium BC), describes how Shennima marries a woman named Gilimninu and promises he won't take a concubine unless she can't have children (*ANET*, 220). Even closer in time to Abraham and Sarah, a tablet from the Old Assyrian period (northern Mesopotamia, 2000–1600 BC) concerns the marriage of Laqipum and Hatala, where he is allowed to take a concubine if she can't have a child within the first two years of their marriage (*ANET*, 192).

Abraham and Sarah continue to falter in their faith. Still, God is not done with them, as we will see in the rest of the story.

23. "The angel of the LORD found Hagar beside a spring of water in the wilderness"

» Gen. 16:7; 16:1–16

This chapter looks at the same passage as the previous one (chap. 22)—namely, Abraham's attempt to produce an heir by taking on a concubine named Hagar. Though Sarah encouraged Abraham to take her, when Hagar becomes pregnant, Sarah harasses her so much that she flees into the wilderness. While in the wilderness, Hagar encounters "the angel of the LORD" (Gen. 16:7, 9). Who is this angel, and what is his relationship to God?

The Hebrew word translated "angel" (*mal'ak*) means "messenger," so it seems the angel of the Lord is one of God's messengers. Interestingly, however, Hagar understands the angel not as one of God's servants but as God himself. In Genesis 16:13, the narrator says, "Hagar used another name to refer to the LORD, who had spoken to her." That name is *'El-ro'i*, which translates as "the God who sees me," and Hagar asks herself in wonder, "Have I truly seen the One who sees me?"

That the angel of the Lord is God himself is also evident in later episodes in Genesis (22:11–18; Exod. 3:2) and elsewhere (e.g., Judg. 13:21–23). This raises a question because God makes it clear that no one can see him and survive. He is too holy and too glorious. Indeed, he tells Moses, "But you may not look directly at my face, for no one may see me and live" (Exod. 33:20). God does, however, allow Moses to see him "from behind" (33:23).

What are we to make of this? God tells Moses that no one can have a full, direct revelation of his glory. But God does make his presence known in indirect ways, and one of those ways appears to be taking on the form of an angel.

Other passages (e.g., Gen. 31:11; 48:16) also feature the angel of the Lord, and even though the context does not make it clear that the angel is the Lord himself, passages like this one make it the best conclusion. Some Christian readers think that these visible human-like appearances of God in the Old Testament are specifically of Jesus, who takes on human form in the New Testament. Such appearances are called Christophanies. However, there are reasons to be skeptical about this understanding. Christ does not take on human form until the time of the incarnation. Since the Bible introduces the trinitarian nature of God slowly over time, no reader of Genesis would have understood the angel of the Lord as an appearance of Jesus, but rather of God himself, who later will reveal himself as having a triune nature.

24. "You will be called Abraham. . . . Her name will be Sarah"

» Gen. 17:5, 15

Throughout the Old Testament, names often carry deep significance for the person and their relationship with God. Sometimes God changes people's names to signify a character change, a new role, or a transition. Genesis 17 gives two examples of such name changes.

The story of the first patriarch revolves around his journey of faith. God has promised that Abram's descendants will be a great nation, yet he has not even had a child with his wife. If there is no child, there will be no nation. Moreover, Abram's wife is getting older, and the hope of a child fades over time. Abram reacts with fear and doubt rather than faith. In Genesis 16, he follows the ancient custom of taking a secondary wife, Hagar, in order to produce an heir, a sure sign that he is losing confidence in God (see chap. 22).

But at the beginning of Genesis 17, God comes again to reassure Abram that he will have a son. In this reassurance, he gives Abram a new name—Abraham—and he explains the significance of the name change. "Abram" in Hebrew means "exalted father," while the name "Abraham" means "father of a multitude." God explains that Abraham will be "the father of a multitude of nations," and further, many kings will descend from him (17:3–7).

As the biblical story continues beyond Genesis, many nations besides Israel (e.g., Ishmaelites, Edomites) will indeed trace their lineage back to Abraham.

God also changes Sarai's name. Here the significance is more subtle. Sarai becomes Sarah, but both names mean "princess." The difference may be dialectical. "Sarai" is how they pronounced "princess" back in Mesopotamia from where they journeyed, while "Sarah" is the way they pronounce the word in Canaan. The slight name change seems to signal that Sarah is now at home not in the land of her origin but in the land that God promised Abraham and his descendants.

25. "Each male among you must be circumcised"

» Gen. 17:10; 17:9–14

Abraham wavers in his faith time and time again. Most recently (see chap. 22 above), he has attempted to gain an heir by taking on a secondary wife, Hagar, and having a son named Ishmael. In Genesis 17 (as in Gen. 15; see chap. 20) God again reassures Abraham that he will fulfill the promise that Abraham will have a son and descendants who will become a great nation (12:2).

In this appearance, God calls Abraham to obey the covenant (Gen. 17:9). He then instructs him to circumcise every male in his household, specifying that this procedure must be performed when the child is eight days old and include every male, whether Abraham's offspring or "foreign-born servants whom you have purchased" (17:12). Any uncircumcised male in the household would "be cut off from the covenant family for breaking the covenant" (17:14). Very significantly, God calls circumcision "a sign of the covenant" between him and Abraham (17:11). What are we to make of all this?

Circumcision involves the cutting off and removal of the foreskin of the penis. God's promise that Abraham will become a great nation involves land and descendants. God says Abraham's descendants will be as numerous as the stars in the sky (Gen. 15:5) and the sand on the seashore (22:17). The word we translate "descendant" in these contexts is the Hebrew word *zera'*, which also means "seed" or "semen." The point is that the covenant with Abraham involves, for men, the male reproductive organ. This is why it is relevant and significant that the "sign" of this particular covenant involves the penis. The ritual involves cutting off the foreskin, the cutting itself being significant to the sign's meaning because someone who was not circumcised would be cut off from the community (17:14). Even those who are circumcised but turn against the Lord are cut off from the community or even executed, as many of the penalties of the law would later suggest.

Most biblical covenants have signs that closely connect with the specific nature of the covenant: the rainbow for the covenant with Noah (Gen. 9:13, see chap. 15), the Sabbath for the covenant with Moses (Exod. 31:13), and here, circumcision for the Abrahamic covenant. Signs function as reminders of the covenant and are supposed to encourage obedience. Circumcision reminded Abraham and his descendants of the covenant, both its promises and its obligations.

26. "He looked up and noticed three men standing nearby"

» Gen. 18:2; 18:1–15

In Genesis 17, God appeared to Abraham to reassure him and to institute circumcision (see chap. 25). He also told Abraham that the promised child would be born within a year (17:21), and Genesis 21 tells of Isaac's birth. Between these chapters in Genesis is one connected story about God's judgment on the wicked cities of Sodom and Gomorrah (Gen. 18–20), and it begins with Abraham receiving three mysterious visitors. The narrator informs the reader that this visit is from "the Lord," that is, Yahweh (18:1).

While the reader knows that the Lord is involved in this visit, it is not clear what Abraham knows. He shows the visitors great respect and rushes to serve them, but nothing he says (notice that he calls one of them "my lord," a title that is appropriate to a human superior) or does indicates that he knows that God is present. He shows them great hospitality, but he also thinks they are just passing through ("let me prepare some food to refresh you before you continue on your journey," Gen. 18:5).

But if Abraham was not aware at that moment that he was receiving a visit from God, it soon became clear. The visitors knew his wife's name, and one of them says he will return in a year and Sarah will have a son. Certainly by this time Abraham and Sarah know that God is with them and is once again reassuring them that they will have the long-awaited son.

What are we to make of the fact that there are three visitors? Christian readers who are aware of the triune nature of the Godhead often take the three visitors to be the Father, the Son, and the Holy Spirit. But such a reading is wrong on a couple of counts. First, while the trinitarian nature of God is an eternal truth, the threefold nature of God is something slowly revealed over time and not really known until the coming of Christ and the revelation of the New Testament. Second, in Genesis 18 one of the figures represents Yahweh (see chap. 23), but the other two are revealed to be angels. We see this when Yahweh sends his two angels into Sodom to rescue Lot and his family from the judgment coming on the city (19:1).

27. "She gave birth to a son for Abraham in his old age"

» Gen. 21:2; 21:1–7

See chapter 28.

28. "Then he tied his son, Isaac, and laid him on the altar on top of the wood"

» Gen. 22:9; 22:1–19

In the previous chapters of Genesis, Abraham struggles with faith as he encounters threats and obstacles to the fulfillment of God's promises, particularly the promise that he would have many descendants. Finally, when he is one hundred years old and Sarah is ninety, Sarah gives birth to Isaac, the child they waited so long for (Gen. 21:1–7). We might ask (as surely Abraham and Sarah would have) why God waited so long. The text does not say, but Abraham and Sarah would have known without a doubt that Isaac was God's gift since they were well beyond the age when humans could have babies. Isaac's birth to previously barren Sarah at her advanced age is one step short of an even more miraculous birth, a virgin birth, that would mark Jesus as God's ultimate gift to humanity.

Readers can be forgiven if they think that the Abraham story has come to its conclusion with the birth of Isaac. From a literary point of view, the tension in the plot has been about the birth. Now that the birth has happened, we expect the text to turn to another topic, but that does not happen.

Rather, some years later (when Isaac is old enough to carry wood; Gen. 22:6), God tells Abraham to "take your son, your only son—yes, Isaac, whom you love so much—and go to the land of Moriah. Go and sacrifice him as a burnt offering on one of the mountains, which I will show you" (22:2). The narrator begins the story by telling us that God was testing Abraham (22:1), but Abraham did not know that it was a test. What we do know is that throughout Abraham's life his faith has been tested and very frequently found wanting. How will he respond to this incredible challenge to his faith?

Surprisingly, he responds with obedience. The narrator does not tell us what Abraham was thinking after God gave this command. He likely was shocked, perhaps even horrified, at the idea of killing his only son, the son of the promise, but his actions show that he trusted God. The very next morning he takes Isaac along with two of his servants and heads toward Moriah.

Contemporary readers are often repulsed by God's command and disgusted by Abraham's compliance, but such a response does not enter into the world of the story or perceive what the narrator chooses to disclose. We already know that the command is a test. We already know that God will not allow Abraham to follow through, or as we will suggest later, that God will raise Isaac from the dead. As we read on, we see that Abraham does not kill Isaac. As for Abraham, the omniscient narrator is not interested in his thoughts; rather, he just describes the patriarch's actions. In this way, the story emphasizes Abraham's utter trust in God at the end of his life in contrast to his wavering faith earlier.

While the Genesis narrator is silent about what Abraham is thinking, we read in Hebrews that "Abraham reasoned that if Isaac died, God was able to bring him back to life again. And in a sense, Abraham did receive his son back from the dead" (Heb. 11:19). In the ancient setting of Genesis, Abraham almost certainly wasn't thinking of the afterlife. He would have thought God would bring Isaac back to life just as, through Elijah, he restored the son of the widow at Zarephath to life (1 Kings 17). Isaac was the promised heir, and Abraham trusted God that Isaac would be heir even if he died.

But Isaac did not die that day on Mount Moriah. Abraham demonstrated his trust in God in a way that had important consequences (see chap. 30 below).

29. "The angel of the LORD called to him from heaven."

» Gen. 22:11

See chapter 23.

30. "I will certainly bless you. . . . all because you have obeyed me"

» Gen. 22:17–18; 22:15–18

In the New Testament, Paul often contests and criticizes theological opponents who argued that we are saved by what we do. Paul pointedly responds that we are justified by faith, and to make this point, he often cites Genesis 15:6: "And Abram believed the Lord, and the Lord counted him as righteous because of his faith" (see Rom. 4:2; Gal. 3:6). Since God pronounced Abraham justified before his circumcision, Abraham's saving relationship with God precedes any works, even the "work" of circumcision in Genesis 17.

In chapter 28 we saw that Abraham obeyed God's command to take Isaac to Mount Moriah to sacrifice him. Abraham did not know this was a test (Gen. 22:1), though what he says on the journey reveals that he hoped God would stay his hand. He tells the two servants who came with them to remain with the donkey while he and Isaac go worship on the mountain, after which, he says, "We will come right back" (22:5). When Isaac asks about the lamb for the sacrifice, Abraham says, "God will provide a sheep for the burnt offering, my son" (22:8).

And God does provide the sacrifice and keeps Abraham from sacrificing his son, even though the passage is clear that Abraham would have followed through with the divine command. As a result, the angel of the Lord, who is the Lord himself (chap. 23), blesses him and says: "I will certainly bless you. I will multiply your descendants beyond number, like the stars in the sky and the sand on the seashore. Your descendants will conquer the cities of their enemies. And through your descendants all the nations of the earth will be blessed—all because you have obeyed me" (Gen. 22:17–18).

God tells Abraham that he will follow through on his promises because of Abraham's obedience. How does this square with

Paul's appeal to Abraham's story to affirm justification by faith? The book of James helps us understand.

James confronts those who think good works are irrelevant to the faith. Those who oppose him say that because we are saved by faith alone, our works are not important. James responds by asking, "What good is it, dear brothers and sisters, if you say you have faith but don't show it by your actions?" (James 2:14). James answers his own question by insisting that "faith without good deeds is useless" (2:20). He justifies his view by paraphrasing Genesis 22 and ends the example by saying, "You see, we are shown to be right with God by what we do, not by faith alone" (2:24).

Does James contradict Paul? Not at all. Like Paul, James cites Genesis 15:6 (James 2:23). But his point is that Abraham's "faith and his actions worked together. His actions made his faith complete" (2:22). In other words, we are not saved by works, but if faith is authentic, then it will result in good works. Good works are the external manifestation of our faith.

Paul believes this as well. For example, Paul imparts to Titus a "trustworthy saying," namely, that Jesus "saved us, not because of the righteous things we had done, but because of his mercy" (Titus 3:5). The result is that "all who trust in God will devote themselves to doing good. These teachings are good and beneficial for everyone" (3:8).

31. "When they mated in front of the white-streaked branches, they gave birth to young that were streaked, speckled, and spotted"

» Gen. 30:39; 30:25–43

Isaac and Rebekah had twin sons, Jacob and Esau. Since Esau came out of the womb first, he was the firstborn and so would have the birthright and his father's blessing. Jacob, encouraged by Rebekah, who had received a message from God that Esau's descendants would serve Jacob's, deceives his father into blessing him and not Esau (Gen. 27:1–28:9).

When Esau realizes what has happened, he goes into a murderous rage. Rebekah tells Jacob to flee to Paddan-Aram and seek refuge with his uncle Laban. When Jacob arrives there, he meets and falls in love with Laban's daughter Rachel. Laban deceives Jacob on his wedding night, substituting Rachel's older sister Leah into his bed. Jacob had worked for seven years to secure Rachel's hand in marriage only to be given Leah, so he works seven more years for Rachel. In many ways, Laban takes advantage of Jacob.

Eventually, Jacob is so wearied by Laban that he decides to go back to the promised land. He asks Laban's permission to take his wives, concubines, and children back home, but Laban knows that his prosperity depends on Jacob. He replies by saying, "Tell me how much I owe you. Whatever it is, I'll pay it" (Gen. 30:28).

Jacob asks Laban to let him have "all the sheep and goats that are speckled or spotted, along with all the black sheep" as his wages (Gen. 30:32). By that identification, Jacob assures Laban, they will clearly be able to differentiate the flocks and there will be no question of ownership or suspicion of theft. But Jacob has an interesting plan in mind.

He takes branches from poplar, almond, and plane trees. He strips the bark, exposing white stripes on the branches. He places these by the watering trough so when Laban's flocks—not spotted, speckled, or striped—mate in front of the stripped branches, their offspring come out streaked, speckled, or spotted, and Jacob could claim them. In addition, he only puts out the branches when the strong animals are at the watering trough. Thus, not only over time did Jacob's flocks increase in number, but they were healthy animals in contrast to the weak or sickly animals in Laban's flock.

What was behind Jacob's plan? Why would animals that were not spotted, speckled, or striped give birth to animals that were?

Genetics don't work that way, so there is no scientific answer to this question. As far as we know, there is no ancient Near Eastern custom that would explain it.

There is no rational explanation. The only answer is that God wanted to increase Jacob's wealth before he returned to his home. Indeed, his increased wealth led to heightened tension between Jacob and Laban and his sons, leading to Jacob and his family stealing away from Laban without telling him.

32. "Then in my dream, the angel of God said to me"

» Gen. 31:11

See chapter 23.

33. "A man came and wrestled with him until the dawn began to break"

» Gen. 32:24; 32:22–32

Having settled matters with Laban, his father-in-law (Gen. 31:22–55), Jacob looks ahead to a potential conflict with Esau. The last time Jacob had seen his brother, Esau wanted to kill him. Accordingly, he sends Esau a message with the hope that he will be well-received or at least not threatened by Esau. When the messengers come back, they give Jacob foreboding news. Esau is on his way with four hundred men—a veritable army.

Jacob plans for the worst. He divides his people and animals into two groups, so if Esau attacks one, the other might get away. He asks God to rescue him from Esau. He then sends Esau waves of gifts with the hope of pacifying him.

After sending his family away, Jacob spends that night alone. Out of nowhere, he is attacked by someone the narrator identifies simply as "a man" (Gen. 32:24). The story of this wrestling match is difficult because the narrator does not tell us much about the identity of the man or his motivation, nor does the narrator interpret or evaluate the action of the story. While such a lack of explanation is not atypical of Hebrew storytelling in general, such information is particularly lacking in this episode. Even so, some matters are clear as we read on.

This man wrestles with Jacob all night, but when the day is about to dawn he tells Jacob he has to leave before the sun comes up (though we are not told why). The man cannot defeat Jacob, so he touches Jacob's hip and dislocates its socket. Jacob will not let the man go unless he blesses Jacob. The man asks for Jacob's name and then changes it to Israel. When Jacob asks the man for his name, he does not give it, but he does bless Jacob.

After the man leaves, Jacob, now Israel, calls the place Peniel ("face of God"). He explains the meaning of that name when he says, "I have seen God face to face, yet my life has been spared" (Gen. 32:30). As readers, we thus learn that the "man" was none other than God. We now know why Jacob wanted the man to bless him.

Of course, this raises other questions. Why couldn't the man defeat Jacob? The best answer is that the man was able to defeat Jacob, but he chose to limit his strength to allow Jacob to engage in a prolonged wrestling match with him. That he could have defeated Jacob can be seen when he is able to dislocate Jacob's hip with a mere touch. Jacob too recognizes that God could have defeated him when he marvels at his survival and knows that he had "been spared" (Gen. 32:30).

It was God's decision to engage Jacob in a struggle over a long period of time when he could have defeated him immediately. He was illustrating to him the struggle that Jacob had engaged in "with God and with men" (Laban, Esau), yet he has overcome these obstacles (Gen. 32:28).

Indeed, the struggle is what causes the name change from Jacob ("one who grabs the ankle," with connotations of "deceiver") to Israel (which means something like "he who struggles with God"). It is a good thing to struggle with and not give up on God. God honors Jacob for it.

What is the significance of the name change? In the first place, a name change shows a change of status, role, or character. In the case of Jacob, it seems to denote a change of character from being a deceptive person, as evident in his earlier interactions with Isaac, Esau, and Laban.

That said, Jacob's character is not completely transformed. In the next part of his life, he engages in deception at least once more when he promises Esau that he will follow him back to his homeland but doesn't (Gen. 33:13–17). He will also greatly damage his family through his favoritism to Rachel and Joseph and then later Benjamin. Perhaps that is why, as opposed to other name changes in the Old Testament (e.g., Abram–Abraham), the narrator will alternate between calling him Jacob and Israel.

The abiding significance of this name change is that Israel will give his name to the future nation. His twelve sons will be the father figures of the twelve tribes that constitute the nation of Israel.

34. "Should we let him treat our sister like a prostitute?"

» Gen. 34:31; 34:1–3

Upon his return from Paddan-Aram to the land of Canaan, Jacob settles in Shechem, a Canaanite city. As a pastoralist, he and his family live on the outskirts of the city, but they still interact with the local inhabitants. One day his daughter Dinah went into town to visit some of her female friends. While she was there, the ruler's son, Shechem, saw her and raped her (Gen. 34:2). The narrator says that the prince "fell in love with her, and he tried to win her affection with tender words" (34:3). He then asked his father, Hamor, to talk to Jacob about marrying his daughter.

Before Hamor could do so, Jacob and his sons heard that Dinah had been violated. The narrator comments that Shechem's actions were something "that should never be done" (Gen. 34:7). The brothers are furious and more so because in the ancient Near East brothers were tasked with keeping their sisters safe.

Still, Hamor makes his pitch for the marriage of his son and Dinah. He asks Jacob to allow Dinah to marry Shechem and even more broadly suggests, "Let's arrange other marriages, too. You give us your daughters for our sons, and we will give you our daughters for your sons. And you may live among us; the land is open to you! Settle here and trade with us. And feel free to buy property in the area" (Gen. 34:9–10). Shechem tells Jacob about his great desire for his daughter.

Dinah's brothers say they will agree to the marriage but only if the men of the city circumcise themselves. The narrator informs us that the brothers were speaking "deceitfully" (Gen. 34:13). We know they are up to something, but we do not know what.

Hamor and his son seize the opportunity and propose the idea to the citizens of the city. They urge them to agree so that the wealthy family of Jacob might be fully integrated into their city. The men find this an attractive opportunity, and so they undergo mass circumcision.

We now learn what lay behind the brothers' plan. Circumcision, the cutting off of the foreskin of the penis, leaves the men of the city in a physically vulnerable position. In addition, the men of Canaan don't expect what comes. Simeon and Levi go through the city, killing all the men. They and the other sons of Jacob pillage the city and take its wealth, as well as "all their little children and wives" (Gen. 34:29).

Jacob, however, is beside himself with anger toward Simeon and Levi. He worries that the reprisal of neighboring people will mean the end of him and his household.

Who in this story, if anyone, has done the right thing? Who does the narrator, the one who represents the perspective of the author and ultimately of God himself, think has done the right thing?

To answer this question, consider who gets the last word in the story. In response to Jacob's anger, Simeon and Levi respond, "Why should we let him treat our sister like a prostitute?" (Gen. 34:31). The narrator appears to sympathize with the brothers. Not only do they defend their sister's honor, but more importantly they prevent the chosen family from intermarrying with pagan Canaanites. To be a blessing to "all the families on earth" (12:3), they need to remain separate from them.

The deed also meant that Jacob and his family had to flee Shechem. But this too is not negative. When Jacob left the promised land for Haran years earlier, God appeared to him at Bethel. Jacob promised that if God allowed him to return, he would make the Lord his God, and he would make the pillar he set up at Bethel God's house and give God a tenth of his wealth (Gen. 28:20–22). So it is finally to Bethel that Jacob goes after being forced out of Shechem.

GENESIS 37-50

The Joseph Story

The last major section of Genesis is often known as the Joseph story or the Joseph narrative. Joseph, the eleventh son of the patriarch Jacob, is the center of attention in these chapters, but the other eleven brothers are also featured, and one entire chapter deals only with Judah and has nothing directly to do with Joseph (Gen. 38; see chap. 35).

The account of Joseph and his eleven brothers is relevant to the future of God's promises to Abraham. These sons of Jacob, renamed Israel, will be the father (or in the case of Joseph, the grandfather) figures of the twelve tribes of Israel. Their actions, particularly those of Joseph and Judah, have implications for their future tribes and the relationships among them.

The story begins as an account of a dysfunctional family. Jacob has eleven sons through his two wives, Leah and Rachel, and two concubines, Bilhah and Zilpah. He makes no secret that his favorite son is Joseph, the long-awaited first son of his favorite wife, Rachel. Jacob gifts Joseph with a "beautiful robe" (Gen. 37:3) and gives him preferential treatment, bringing on the animosity of his brothers.

Joseph does not help the situation. He has two dreams, which he interprets publicly to his brothers as indicating his superior status. He is right that he will have a special role to play, but it will involve suffering and service to his family, not special privilege.

With this background the narrator recounts a time when Jacob sends Joseph to check on his brothers as they have taken the flocks to pasture far from home (Gen. 37:12–36). When his brothers see him from a distance, they plot how to get rid of him. They consider killing him and disposing of his body, but Reuben, the eldest, convinces them to throw Joseph into a cistern instead, presumably to leave him there. Reuben secretly plans to return to the cistern and get him out. However, while he is away, the other brothers see a caravan of traders heading toward Egypt. They, under the leadership of Judah, decide to get rid of Joseph and profit at the same time by selling him to the traders, who take him to Egypt and sell him as a slave.

The story focuses on Joseph, but Reuben and especially Judah get special attention in ways that have implications for their later tribes. Reuben, the firstborn, shows himself here and elsewhere to be inept. Judah plays a negative role at first, not only in suggesting the sale of Joseph here but also later when he marries a Canaanite and impregnates his daughter-in-law (Gen. 38; see chap. 35). But Judah will undergo transformation to become a self-sacrificial leader. These threads of the Joseph story help explain why later the tribe of Judah, and not the tribe of Reuben, becomes a dominant force in Israel along with Ephraim, one of the Joseph tribes.

As the story continues, Joseph becomes the slave of a high Egyptian official named Potiphar. He assumes great responsibility in the household, and Potiphar's estate flourishes as a result (Gen. 39). However, Potiphar's wife tries to seduce and then force Joseph into a sexual tryst, and when he resists, she frames him so he is thrown in jail.

But the jail then flourishes with Joseph's presence. When two of his fellow prisoners, the chief cupbearer and the chief baker, have disturbing dreams, Joseph interprets them. He tells the cupbearer that his dream foresees his release from prison and return to Pharaoh's good graces, but he informs the baker that he will be beheaded and impaled. When the cupbearer leaves the prison, as Joseph said he would, Joseph asks him to intercede on his behalf.

The chief cupbearer forgets about Joseph until Pharaoh himself has disturbing dreams. At the cupbearer's recommendation, Pharaoh brings Joseph to court from prison. Joseph interprets the dreams as foretelling seven years of plenty followed by seven years of famine. Pharaoh then elevates Joseph to a very high position in court and tells him to prepare the nation for the famine (Gen. 41).

The famine not only hits Egypt but the surrounding area hard, including Canaan where Jacob and his remaining eleven sons live. In Genesis 42, the narrative turns to Canaan, where Jacob tells ten sons to journey to Egypt and get grain. However, Jacob would not let his new favorite son, Benjamin, take the potentially perilous trip.

The family's need takes the brothers to Joseph himself, who recognizes them. They do not recognize him because he looks, talks, and acts like an Egyptian. Joseph quickly devises a test to see if the brothers have changed since they sold him into slavery (see chap. 36). He accuses them of lying and coming to spy in Egypt. They have already told him about Benjamin back home, so he tells them to verify their story by bringing Benjamin to him. In the meantime, he keeps Simeon in Egypt. Joseph sends them home with grain, and without their knowledge, he puts their money back in their sacks. When they later discover the money, they are confused and frightened.

The brothers return home to Jacob, who is upset at their report and refuses to let Benjamin go with them. But when the family runs out of grain again, Judah takes responsibility for Benjamin (for more on Judah's role in the story, see chap. 36).

The brothers return to Egypt with Benjamin. Joseph releases Simeon and sends them on their way with more grain. However, Joseph continues to test them, this time by framing Benjamin for the theft of his diviner's cup (see chap. 36). Now the brothers have to decide whether to give Benjamin up, as they earlier had done with Joseph, or stand up for him. Judah asks to take his place. At this point, Joseph knows they have changed and reveals himself to them. He tells them to go back and get Jacob, and the family is reunited in Egypt.

After Jacob dies, the brothers fear that Joseph will finally punish them. They offer themselves to him as servants, but he tells them, "You intended to harm me, but God intended it all for good. He brought me to this position so I could save the lives of many people" (Gen. 50:20). At the end of his life Joseph could look back on his suffering and see that it brought him to a place where he could save not only the Egyptian people but also his own family.

35. "She is more righteous than I am, because I didn't arrange for her to marry my son Shelah"

» Gen. 38:26; 38:1–30

The last part of Genesis (Gen. 37–50) centers on Joseph, who is clearly the main character. His brothers come into the story only as they interact with Joseph, and when they do, they usually act as a group. There is one exception to this, Genesis 38, which concerns Judah and him alone apart from all the other brothers.

Scholars have often wondered why Genesis 38 exists in the Joseph narrative. Some even suggest that it doesn't belong there, that it intrudes into the story. Such a view, however, comes from too narrow an understanding of these final chapters, a misunderstanding that might arise in part because we tend to think of this section only as the story of Joseph.

However, the introduction to this final section of Genesis does not say, "This is the account of Joseph." Rather, it says, "This is the account of Jacob and his family" (Gen 37:2). Joseph may be the main character, but these chapters are actually about all the sons of Jacob. Among the other sons, Judah will be the most important because of the leading role that the tribe bearing his name will later play. Genesis 38 helps us get to know who Judah is at the beginning of the story.

What we learn is not pretty. We already know Judah is not virtuous from his introduction in Genesis 37, where Jacob sends Joseph to check on his brothers who were shepherding their flock near a city called Dothan. The brothers hate Joseph because their father favors him. When they see him coming, their first thought is to kill him. Instead, they throw him in a pit.

Reuben, the firstborn, should have interceded immediately, but he demonstrates a lack of courage and leadership by planning to secretly free Joseph later. But while Reuben is away, it is Judah who suggests selling him to traders en route to Egypt.

With this background to Judah, Genesis 38 recounts events after he has moved away from his family and is staying with a local inhabitant named Hirah. He should not be mingling with Canaanites, though, because God's chosen family was to remain separate so they could bring a blessing to the nations (12:3). To make matters even worse, Judah marries a Canaanite woman and has three sons with her: Er, Onan, and Shelah.

He marries his firstborn son to a Canaanite woman named Tamar (Gen. 38:6). But Er was evil, "so the LORD took his life" (38:7). During Old Testament times, if a man died before his wife had a child, a brother or close relative was responsible to marry his widow and father children for her (Deut. 25:5–10; see chap. 104). Otherwise, the childless widow would have no one to care for her in that ancient society (remember the story of Ruth).

Accordingly, when Er died, Judah ordered his second son to fulfill his duty to Tamar and marry her (Gen. 38:8). The narrator then takes us into the bedroom and the mind of Onan, who "spilled the semen on the ground" because he did not want to raise a child that was not his own (38:9). For this sin, God judged him and he died.

Judah's first two sons died because they were evil, but Judah begins to blame Tamar. He should have arranged to give his third son to Tamar as a husband, but the narrator says Judah had no plans to do so because he was afraid Shelah might also die. Judah tells Tamar that Shelah needs to get older before they marry, but the reader knows Judah never intends this marriage to happen.

Tamar returns to her father's house to wait for Judah to send Shelah to her. She waits and waits, and of course nothing happens. So she decides to take matters into her own hands.

One day when Judah goes with his friend Hirah to the city of Timnah to shear his sheep, he sees a prostitute along the road. Not knowing it is Tamar dressed to deceive, he says he wants to sleep with her. He promises to send her a young goat as payment, but she insists on collateral in advance of payment. He gives her his "seal and its cord" and his "walking stick" (38:18), objects of identification.

Judah sleeps with his daughter-in-law Tamar, to him an anonymous prostitute. When he returns to pay her, she cannot be found. His friend Hirah asks a group of people if they have seen a shrine prostitute around, and they answer, "We've never had a shrine prostitute here" (Gen. 38:21). While there were prostitutes in the employ of the fertility cults, there is no earlier indication that Tamar presented herself as such. It may be that the friend asked specifically for a shrine prostitute to make the situation look more respectable than it was. In any case, when he returns to Judah, Judah decides he has done his best and does not want to look like a "laughingstock" (38:23).

About three months later, Judah hears that Tamar is pregnant. He simply announces, "Let her be burned" (Gen. 38:24). But as they bring her out to be burned, she takes out the seal, cord, and staff and says the owner of these objects is the father. Judah then realizes he is the man, admitting, "She is more righteous than

I am, because I didn't arrange for her to marry my son Shelah" (38:26).

What is the purpose of this story that only concerns Judah and not Joseph and the other brothers? It provides additional confirmation of Judah's sinful character and behavior. Judah will be the second most important character in the Joseph narrative, and the narrative will show Judah later in his life in contrast to the Judah seen here. He will offer himself in place of an endangered Benjamin, and as a transformed man he will assume leadership among the brothers and receive his father's blessing of a ruling role for the tribe that descends from him (see chaps. 36 and 39).

36. "Why have you stolen my master's silver cup?"

» Gen. 44:5; 42:1–44:34

In Genesis 44, Joseph frames his brother Benjamin for stealing his silver diviner's cup and threatens to make him his slave. Some people read this episode and question Joseph's morality. He frames his brother? And what is he doing with a diviner's cup, a device used to perform a ritual that compels the gods to reveal the future?

A little background not only alleviates Joseph of wrongdoing but shows the wisdom of his actions. First, remember that Joseph's ten older brothers had sold Joseph into slavery in Egypt. They did not know that a number of divinely guided experiences had made Joseph Pharaoh's right-hand man and the one in charge of crisis management in the face of an enduring famine (see Gen. 50:19–20). Joseph had taken on Egyptian clothing and customs, so the brothers after many years did not recognize him when they came for grain to survive the famine (Gen. 42). Benjamin did not accompany the ten brothers because he had replaced Joseph as Jacob's favorite. Benjamin was the youngest, and to Jacob's knowledge, he was Rachel's only surviving son.

When the ten brothers approach Joseph to ask for grain, they simply think he is a powerful Egyptian official. Joseph does not reveal his identity to them, and who can blame him after what they did to him? Have they changed? Can they be trusted?

He interrogates them, though he knows the answer to most of the questions. "Where are you from?" They respond, "From the land of Canaan" (Gen. 42:7). He then accuses them of being spies. They vehemently deny the charge. As they defend themselves, they reveal that they left a younger brother (Benjamin) at home with their father.

Joseph then tests them for the first time. He gives them grain to take back but demands that one of them stay in Egypt as a hostage until they bring the younger brother to him to verify their story. Simeon stays. Without the brothers' knowledge, Joseph has the silver they paid for the grain placed back in their sacks. When they later discover it, they are afraid, thinking they will be considered thieves (Gen. 42:28).

When Jacob hears what happened, he refuses to let them take Benjamin to Egypt. He is upset because that means Simeon is lost to him, but Benjamin is the prized son now. Reuben, the firstborn, steps forward with the inane offer that if they go down with Benjamin and do not return him to Jacob, then Jacob can put Reuben's two sons to death (Gen. 42:37), as if losing two of his grandsons would appeal to Jacob.

But after a while the grain runs out again. If the brothers don't get more, they will all die. This time Judah, not the incompetent Reuben, steps forward and tells his father that he will be personally responsible for Benjamin's safety (Gen. 43:8–9). Jacob reluctantly agrees and advises them how to approach the man, not knowing it is Joseph.

When the brothers arrive back in Egypt, Joseph advises his steward to treat them well. In response to their anxiety about the silver, the steward tells them that he had indeed received payment and their God must have put it back in their sacks with the grain (Gen. 43:23). Joseph then has them fed, amazing them by seating them in birth order. They are even more amazed that

Benjamin receives five times the portions they do. They do not know yet that they are dealing with Joseph.

In Genesis 44, as the brothers leave for home, Joseph gives his steward further instructions. He is to give them grain, again return their silver, and also put Joseph's "personal silver cup" in Benjamin's sack (44:2). Joseph has set a trap to discover whether his brothers have changed from long ago when they sold him into slavery. Will they sacrifice their father's favorite, Benjamin, to save themselves, and so demonstrate that they are not concerned about their father's feelings?

After the brothers have left, Joseph sends his steward after them to spring the trap. When he does, he "discovers" the silver cup in Benjamin's sack and follows Joseph's instructions, asking, "Why have you stolen my master's silver cup, which he uses to predict the future?" (Gen. 44:5). In despair, the brothers return to Joseph, who demands, "What have you done? Don't you know that a man like me can predict the future?" (44:15). The brothers' conscience is pricked by their past sin against Joseph, and Judah declares, "God is punishing us for our sins" (44:16). Judah offers all of them to be Joseph's slaves, but Joseph says that only Benjamin will be his slave and the rest can return home.

Here Joseph's wisdom becomes clear. He has set up an analogous situation to the one that brought him to Egypt in the first place. The now-favored son of Jacob, Benjamin, is at risk of slavery in Egypt. The brothers can rescue themselves and get rid of another favorite, but they refuse to do so, showing Joseph that they have indeed changed. Joseph then reveals his true identity, and so begins the process of reconciliation and also the survival of the family of God through a devastating famine.

As for the divination cup, that is harder to answer. Did Joseph engage in divinatory practices that were later condemned in Scripture (Deut. 18:9–13)? Was it part of his Egyptian ruse along with adopting Egyptian dress? We cannot say for certain, but its purpose in the story is simply to frame Benjamin.

37. "Joseph bought all the land of Egypt for Pharaoh."

» Gen. 47:20; 47:13–31

The Joseph story chronicles how the descendants of Abraham survived a devastating famine and ended up in Egypt, where many centuries later God will rescue them from bondage and forced labor (Exod. 1–15). Joseph's brothers sold him into slavery in Egypt out of their jealousy that he was Jacob's favorite, but God uses this for good, for the saving of many people (Gen. 50:19–20) as Joseph rises from slavery to a position where he can manage the famine on Pharaoh's behalf. His management begins with storing grain during the seven years of plenty that precede the seven years of famine. While we are most interested in how Joseph's wisdom results in the survival of Jacob and his family, this chapter considers the significance of his work on behalf of Pharaoh and the Egyptian people.

When the famine begins, Joseph starts selling grain to the people of Egypt and to "people from all around" (Gen. 41:56–57). His plan benefits Egypt and the surrounding nations. We should read his wise planning and actions as an example of how Abraham and his descendants would be a blessing to "all the families on earth" (12:3). Right after Joseph provides food for money, the story turns to Jacob's family in Canaan (42:1–47:12).

Genesis 47:13–26 returns attention to the famine in Egypt, where the situation has only continued and grown worse for the Egyptians. Stored grain is still available, but the people have run out of money to buy it. In response, Joseph requires first their livestock and then their land as payment. The narrative reports that "Joseph bought all the land of Egypt for Pharaoh" (47:20). He "made them all slaves, from one end of Egypt to another" (47:21). He allows them to work the land they no longer own but requires them to give 20 percent of their crops to Pharaoh.

Is this still an example of God blessing all peoples on earth through Abraham's descendants? The people themselves recognize that Joseph has saved their lives (Gen. 47:25), so perhaps so. But he also put them in bondage to Pharaoh in order to do it.

By enriching the throne and granting it autocratic powers, Joseph also sets the stage for a future pharaoh to enslave the Israelites. Remembering that the book of Genesis was written after the exodus makes us wonder how a postexodus Israelite community would read this story. A definite answer is hard to come by. They may have considered their enslaver to be an ingrate, considering that Joseph's actions had given him such wealth and power. Perhaps too the story might justify the wealth that the freed Israelites carried out of Egypt (Exod. 11:2–3; 12:35–36). It's difficult to be dogmatic about the ethics of Joseph's actions here, but ultimately, as with the actions of his brothers, God used it for good for the people of God.

38. "The angel who has redeemed me from all harm"

» Gen. 48:16

See chapter 23.

39. "I will tell you what will happen to each of you in the days to come"

» Gen. 49:1; 49:1–12

At the end of his life, Jacob issues blessings or curses on his twelve sons, pronouncements that have consequences for the future tribes that descend from them. Jacob's other name is Israel, and the twelve tribes that constitute future Israel descend from his sons (with two tribes fathered by the sons of Joseph, Ephraim and Manasseh; see Gen. 48).

Two of the most consequential pronouncements concern Levi and Simeon (Gen. 49:5–7), who are treated together, and Judah (49:8–12). Jacob pronounces a dire fate for the former and a blessed state for the latter. Both futures come to pass but perhaps not exactly as Jacob intended.

Jacob starts with his firstborn, Reuben, and then works through the birth order. He castigates Reuben for sleeping with Jacob's concubine (Gen. 35:22), and so he "will be first no longer" (49:4). That is, the tribe associated with him will not assume leadership among the tribes. Simeon and Levi are the second- and third-born sons. Jacob begins by recalling their actions in Shechem, where they orchestrated the massacre of the inhabitants of that town in retribution for the violation of their sister. Jacob was angry with them then (see chap. 34) and still is. He thus curses them and declares, "I will scatter them among the descendants of Jacob; I will disperse them throughout Israel" (49:7). This curse looks forward to the future distribution of the promised land to the various tribes, when the descendants of both Simeon (Josh. 19:1–9) and Levi (Josh. 21) will not receive a tribal allotment of land. Rather they are given cities within other tribes. The intended result of the scattering is that they will lose their distinctive tribal identity and eventually be absorbed into other tribes. This happens to Simeon, but because of the Levites' actions at the time of the golden calf (Exod. 32), they, though scattered, become the most distinctive of all tribes in Israel (see chap. 64).

This disqualification of the first three sons leads to Jacob's blessing of the fourth-born, Judah. Jacob indicates that Judah will become the leader among the tribes. Judah will receive the praise of his brothers, the other tribes. He will be powerful and dangerous to his enemies ("like a lion," Gen. 49:9). Perhaps the most striking comment about the future of Judah comes when Jacob announces:

> The scepter will not depart from Judah,
>   nor the ruler's staff from his descendants,
> until the coming of the one to whom it belongs,
>   the one whom all nations will honor. (Gen. 49:10)

The scepter and the ruler's staff are symbols of kingship. In this blessing, Jacob pronounces that Judah will be the preeminent tribe, and from this tribe will come the king. Christians often assume this is a prophecy of Jesus, who is the anointed king, and ultimately it is. But more immediately, the promise is for kingship over Israel, a promise fulfilled when David of the tribe of Judah becomes the king of Israel and God enters into a covenant with him that ensures he will have a son on the throne forever (2 Sam. 7). Jesus is the son of David and thus the complete fulfillment of the promise of kingship.

EXODUS 1-18

Exodus from Egypt

The book of Genesis ends with the account of Joseph's death (Gen. 50:22–26). Just before he died, he "made the sons of Israel swear an oath" that they must take his bones away from Egypt and back to the promised land. A lengthy but indeterminate time elapses between the end of Genesis and the opening of Exodus, where conditions have changed dramatically. First, rather than being simply a large family, the Israelites are now a numerous people. Second, a new king has arisen in Egypt "who knew nothing about Joseph or what he had done" (Exod. 1:8). This king is suspicious of a large foreign people living in the midst of his country, so he consigns them to "crushing labor" to build the store cities of Pithom and Rameses (1:11). He also attempts to reduce the threat by ordering that Hebrew male babies be killed at birth (see chap. 40).

Exodus 2 turns to a Levite couple. The woman gives birth to a child that God will use to lead Israel out of Egypt—Moses. Because of Pharaoh's edict to kill Hebrew male babies, Moses's parents hide him until he gets too big. Moses's mother then puts him in a papyrus basket and places him on the Nile River (see chap. 41). Of all people, Pharaoh's own daughter finds him, and she raises him in the shadow of the king, while his Hebrew mother acts as his wet nurse.

When Moses grows up, however, he sees an Egyptian taskmaster abusing a Hebrew, and he kills the Egyptian. Though he thinks no one has seen him, the word gets out, and he flees the country. He goes to Midian, where he joins a tribal leader (Reuel/Jethro), marries his daughter Zipporah, and settles there as a shepherd.

One day while shepherding in the wilderness, Moses sees a bush on fire, but the flames don't consume the bush. As Moses approaches, God speaks from the bush, commissioning Moses to return to Egypt (see chap. 42) and demand that Pharaoh release the Israelites from slavery. God reveals his name to Moses, and after a series of protests, Moses submits to God's call and departs for Egypt with his family. On the way, Moses has an enigmatic and dangerous encounter with God (see chap. 43). When he finally gets to Egypt, Moses first demands that Pharaoh allow the Israelites to go into the wilderness for three days to worship God (see chap. 44). Pharaoh refuses because his heart is hard (see chap. 45). Eventually Moses demands that Pharaoh free the Israelites unconditionally. Each time Pharaoh refuses the demand, God sends a more intense plague. These plagues attack not just the Egyptians and their leaders but the very gods they worship (see chap. 46). The tenth plague, the death of the firstborn, finally breaks through Pharaoh's hard heart, and he orders the Israelites to leave.

However, after they leave, Pharaoh's heart once again hardens, and he leads his elite chariot troops against the Israelites, camped by the Red Sea. When the Egyptians attack, Moses extends his walking stick, a symbol of God's presence, over the waters, causing them to divide and allowing the Israelites to escape. The Egyptians follow, but God closes the sea on them. The Israelites are finally free from Egyptian bondage, and they begin their trek across the wilderness toward the promised land. The exodus with its crossing of the sea is the preeminent salvation event in the Old Testament.

40. "But because the midwives feared God, they refused to obey the king's orders"

» Exod. 1:17; 1:15–22

When the book of Exodus begins, the chosen family has "multiplied so greatly that they became extremely powerful and filled the land" (Exod. 1:7). Their growth reminds us of the divine promise that Abraham's descendants would become a great nation, but at the moment they are residents in the land of Egypt. When a "new king . . . who knew nothing about Joseph or what he had done" (1:8) rises to power, he grows anxious about the presence of a large foreign people in the midst of his kingdom. He enslaves the Israelites, making them work on building the cities of Pithom and Rameses (1:11). Even so, the Israelites continue to grow, only increasing the pharaoh's anxiety.

The pharaoh devises a new strategy to weaken what he considers a potential internal threat. He summons the "Hebrew midwives, Shiphrah and Puah" (Exod. 1:15), and orders them to kill any baby boy born to the Israelites.

This text raises questions for modern readers that are hard to answer because they are not issues that interested the ancient author. First, the narrator calls these women "Hebrew midwives," but it is not clear whether they are Hebrew themselves or whether they are midwives to the Hebrews. Although they have Semitic-sounding names, it's probably the latter. Indeed, contemporary Jewish culture often celebrates them as "righteous gentiles." Second, that there are only two midwives for all of Israel seems odd. Either these two are in charge of the midwives or, more likely, Israel is not as big as we sometimes imagine.

These are peripheral issues in which the author has no interest. The real question has to do with the midwives' actions and speech to Pharaoh. They refuse to follow through on Pharaoh's command to kill the baby boys, and they lie to him about it. Rather than owning up to their actions, they cover them up by saying, "The Hebrew women are not like the Egyptian women. They are more vigorous and have their babies so quickly that we cannot get there in time" (Exod. 1:19). Some readers believe that even if the results are good, the means are wrong. After all, the ninth commandment prohibits lying: "You must not testify falsely against your neighbor" (20:16).

The question is, Did the midwives break the ninth commandment as they saved the lives of Hebrew baby boys? Rarely do Hebrew narrators, who represent the perspective of the biblical authors, explicitly evaluate the morality of characters, but they do send subtle signals as to whether they approve or disapprove. In the story of the midwives, the signals are decisive that God enthusiastically approved of the midwives' actions: "So God was good to the midwives, and the Israelites continued to multiply, growing more and more powerful. And because the midwives feared God, he gave them families of their own" (Exod. 1:20–21). Their motivation was their fear of God, and God heartily rewarded them.

The narratives of Scripture will often help us interpret the didactic or legal sections of Scripture. What does this story teach us? There are occasions when lying is not only permissible, but not to lie is a sin. When are those occasions? In this case, lying is appropriate when one knows that the person asking for the truth wants to use it to harm others. Their reason for knowing the truth—that is, hurting others—means they forfeit the right to the truth.

41. "She got a basket made of papyrus reeds and waterproofed it"

» Exod. 2:3; 2:1–10

Pharaoh issued a decree to kill all the Hebrew baby boys because he feared the growing population of Hebrews in his country threatened national security. After the Hebrew midwives resisted his demand to kill baby boys as they came out of the womb (see chap. 40), he called on all Egyptians to kill newborn Hebrew boys by throwing them into the Nile River (Exod. 1:22).

Accordingly, when a Levite couple named Amran and Jochebed have a baby boy, the mother tries to keep it a secret. However, the boy grows enough that it becomes impossible to hide him. Jochebed devises a plan to save her baby's life even if she cannot raise him. This baby is Moses.

Jochebed makes a basket out of papyrus reeds and uses tar and pitch to waterproof it. She places baby Moses in the basket and then places it on the Nile River. The baby's sister, Miriam, watches from nearby to see what will happen to the boy in the basket.

Eventually, the basket is spotted by none other than Pharaoh's own daughter, who recognizes that the baby is a Hebrew. Miriam emerges and offers to find a wet nurse for the baby, who turns out to be Moses's own mother. Jochebed takes her baby home, nurses him, and eventually brings him to the palace to be raised by Pharaoh's daughter, who calls him Moses. According to the narrator, Moses's name derives from this event, as Pharaoh's daughter "lifted him out of the water"—presumably the name sounds something like the Hebrew verb "to lift out" (Exod. 2:10). But since it is unlikely the Egyptian princess spoke Hebrew or gave her son a Hebrew name, it is more likely that the name connects to an Egyptian word that means "born." (The name of the fifteenth-century Egyptian pharaoh Thutmoses means "born of [the god] Thoth.") The biblical narrator is making a meaningful and playful connection with the Hebrew.

This passage drips with ironic reversals. Pharaoh wants Hebrew babies thrown into the Nile, which Moses's mother does, but in a reed basket. The baby was supposed to die at Pharaoh's command but ends up being raised by his very own daughter. The reason for Pharaoh's decree was his fear of insurrection, and that insurrection will be led by this child raised in his own house. Not only does Moses's mother save her child from death, she also gets to nurse him (and gets paid for her work). Finally, at the end of the story, it is Pharoah's army that gets thrown into the sea.

To the modern reader, the idea of putting a baby in a basket and placing it on the river seems outlandish, the stuff of legend or fairy tales. Interestingly, another ancient Near Eastern story tells of a mother, in this case a high priestess, who puts her son in a basket and places him on the Tigris River. We don't know why she does this, but probably because, for some reason (perhaps because she is a high priestess), she should not have a baby. Her baby, the future king Sargon, is picked up by an irrigation ditch digger who raises the boy as his own. While some have argued that the Moses story mimics the Sargon birth story, the better explanation is that both stories represent one way that women who could not keep their children but wanted them to live could commit them not to the chance of the river currents but rather to their deity's care.

42. "I AM WHO I AM"

» Exod. 3:14; 3:13–15

Moses's encounter with God at the burning bush is one of the most significant events in Old Testament history. Moses was born to a couple from the tribe of Levi (Exod. 2:1; Num. 26:59). Due to Pharaoh's decree to kill baby boys born to the Hebrews, Moses's parents had placed Moses in a basket and floated it down the Nile where it was found by Pharaoh's daughter. Thus, Moses, the future leader of Israel's rescue from Egyptian bondage, would be raised in the very household of Pharaoh (see chap. 41).

When Moses grows up, he goes out to see his own people, the Hebrews. He knows he is a Hebrew (Exod. 2:11), even though we can't be certain how he learned about his heritage. Perhaps his mother, who had been hired to nurse him, still had connections with him when he was old enough to be aware, or perhaps the Egyptian princess informed him. When he witnesses an Egyptian abusing a Hebrew worker, he kills him. Though he tries to cover up the crime by burying the Egyptian in the sand, word gets out, and Moses knows he has to flee Egypt. Whatever status he has will not protect him from the consequences of the crime.

He flees to the region of Midian and enters into the service of a local shepherd named Jethro (also known as Reuel; Exod. 2:18, 20), who is described as "the priest of Midian" (3:1). Moses marries one of Jethro's daughters, Zipporah, and likely expects this is how he will live the rest of his days.

Then he encounters God. While out with the flock, Moses sees a bush on fire but not being consumed by the flames. As he approaches, a voice calls to him: "Moses! Moses!" (Exod. 3:4). The voice commands that he remove his sandals because the ground is holy. The voice then identifies itself to Moses as "the God of Abraham, the God of Isaac, and the God of Jacob" (3:6). God informs Moses that he knows about the suffering of his people in Egypt. Then he instructs Moses to "lead my people out of Egypt" (3:10).

Moses balks at the command, protesting his inability to assume such a mammoth responsibility. But God assures Moses that he himself will accompany him to Egypt.

Up to this point, the narrative has been straightforward, but matters get a bit more complex for modern readers when Moses asks for God's name. Yes, he is the God of the Hebrews' ancestors, but when the people ask for God's name, Moses wonders, "What should I tell them?" (Exod. 3:13).

The first issue is whether or not the name God gives is new. The name is Yahweh, and we will consider its meaning below, but was this the first time Moses or the Israelites had heard it? Perhaps, but then how would that reassure the people in the way Moses hopes? Second, the book of Genesis uses the name Yahweh before this time. While the name occurs mostly in the narrative, sometimes one of the characters uses it as well (e.g., Gen. 4:1; 9:26; cf. 13:4). Genesis is told from a post–burning bush perspective, so it is possible that the later storyteller used "Yahweh" where the historical character used another name for God.

The bottom line is that we can't be sure. Even so, we can understand the importance of this moment whether it is an initial revelation of the name or, more likely, a deeper awareness of the name's significance.

God responds first with a sentence (*'ehyeh 'asher 'ehyeh*) translated by the NLT as "I AM WHO I AM," with a footnote giving the alternative "I WILL BE WHAT I WILL BE." The word repeated twice is a first-person imperfect of the verb *hayah*, "to be." Hebrew does not have tense, and the imperfect indicates an incomplete action or state of being, which can be rendered in English as either present or future. Whichever it is, the significance is that God through his name asserts his independence. He is not defined by anyone but himself.

But this initial sentence is more an explanation of the name than the name itself. The name itself is another form of the verb "to be." In the original Hebrew it has no vowels but is represented by four consonants (sometimes called the tetragrammaton, meaning "four letters"), YHWH.

Jewish scribes during the Middle Ages (the Masoretes) added vowels to the consonantal text to aid with reading. When pronounced with these vowels, the name sounds like Yehovah, which often gets written in English as Jehovah. But that is almost certainly not how it was originally pronounced. The Masoretes believed it was sacrilegious to actually pronounce God's name, so they gave it the vowels from the Hebrew word *'adonai*, which means "lord," and thus many English translations render YHWH as "the Lord." The much more likely transliteration of the name is *Yahweh*. That is God's personal name, and here in Exodus Yahweh is both identifying the name with the way he made himself known as the God of Abraham, Isaac, and Jacob and informing Moses of the name's significance.

43. "You are a bridegroom of blood to me"

» Exod. 4:25; 4:24–31

One of the most enigmatic texts of the Old Testament describes an event when Moses journeys to Egypt from Midian after his commission to lead the Hebrews out of Egypt (Exod. 4:18–26). His wife Zipporah and his sons are traveling with him.

One night after the family has settled down for the evening, God suddenly "was about to kill him" (Exod. 4:24). It is not exactly clear who he is trying to kill—Moses or one of his sons—nor does the narrator give a reason why God would want to do this.

Zipporah quickly takes action. With a flint knife, she circumcises her son. She then takes the foreskin and touches "his feet" (probably a euphemism for his genitals) with it. Here, "his" seems to refer to Moses because she then pronounces, "Now you are a bridegroom of blood to me" (Exod. 4:25). The narrator explains that by "bridegroom of blood" Zipporah refers to circumcision. Then the narrator simply concludes the story—"After that, the Lord left him alone" (4:26)—and moves on to the next story with nothing more to say about this incident.

A reader might be forgiven for wondering what in the world just happened. God had commissioned Moses to go and bring his people out of Egypt, and now he tries to kill him (or his son). The son gets circumcised, God leaves him alone, and the incident is not spoken of again. What are we to make of this?

First, we must acknowledge that there are lots of questions we can't answer. But one point is clear: Circumcision is important to Yahweh. We might wonder why Moses's son had not yet been circumcised as he should have been on the eighth day (see Gen. 17:9–14). Maybe Zipporah, who was a Midianite, was not in favor of it. Her harsh reaction to Moses may indicate this, but surely Moses should have known better. Perhaps this incident led to conflict in the relationship. The next and only other time we hear about Zipporah, the narrator reports that Moses had sent her and his two sons back to Midian, most likely at this time (Exod. 18:3). Moses would be reunited with his family as he passed through Midian on his way to the promised land. But again, with all the ambiguities of this story, we should not lose sight of the importance God places on the ritual of circumcision (for which see chap. 25).

44. "Let us take a three-day journey into the wilderness"

» Exod. 5:3; 5:1–5

God commissioned Moses to lead his people out of their Egyptian bondage to Pharaoh and take them to the promised land, a "fertile and spacious land. . . . a land flowing with milk and honey" (Exod. 3:8). Perhaps a bit surprisingly then, when Moses first confronts Pharaoh, he does not ask that Pharaoh let the people go permanently. Rather, Moses and Aaron quote God as saying, "Let my people go so they may hold a festival in my honor in the wilderness" (5:1). Pharaoh scoffs at the request, but then Moses and Aaron say, "The God of the Hebrews has met with us. . . . So let us take a three-day journey into the wilderness so we can offer sacrifices to the Lord our God" (5:3).

How do we account for the discrepancy? What if Pharaoh had granted the request? Would they have gone to the wilderness for three days and returned as they had said? Would they have kept going, having bought themselves a three-day head start?

First, we have to acknowledge that God is in on this initial request. Though he clearly says the ultimate goal is for the Hebrews to leave Egypt permanently and return to the promised land, he is the one who tells Moses to go to Pharaoh and say, "The Lord, the God of the Hebrews, has met with us. So please let us take a three-day journey into the wilderness to offer sacrifices to the Lord, our God" (Exod. 3:18).

Why? God does not explicitly state his motive, but Exodus 3:19–22 offers a strong indication of his rationale:

> But I know that the king of Egypt will not let you go unless a mighty hand forces him. So I will raise my hand and strike the Egyptians, performing all kinds of miracles among them. Then at last he will let you go. And I will cause the Egyptians to look favorably on you. They will give you gifts when you go so you will not leave empty-handed. Every Israelite woman will ask for articles of silver and gold and fine clothing from her Egyptian neighbors and from the foreign women in their houses. You will dress your sons and daughters with these, stripping the Egyptians of their wealth.

God knows that Pharaoh will refuse even this relatively minor request, showing his stubbornness (hard heart, see chap. 45). His refusal will lead to God sending the plagues that will bring judgment on Pharaoh, the Egyptian people, and the gods of Egypt (see chap. 46). This judgment will give glory to God (Exod. 14:4). By the time God is done with them, the Egyptians will not only let God's people go permanently but will also give them gifts (12:34–36).

Events transpire just as expected. Moses and Aaron ask that the Hebrews be allowed to go to the wilderness for three days to worship the Lord, and Pharaoh denies their request. In addition, Pharaoh decides to increase the people's suffering by forcing them not only to make the bricks for construction but to gather the straw needed to make the bricks. Initially, the people are upset with Moses for making their condition worse, but God informs Moses that he "will see what I will do to Pharaoh. When he feels the force of my strong hand, he will let the people go. In fact, he will force them to leave his land!" (Exod. 6:1). Thus begin the plagues that steadily increase in intensity with each demand. At first, Moses keeps repeating the request for a three-day break to worship God, and at one point Pharaoh agrees, only to renege on the agreement (8:25–32). Even though Pharaoh keeps refusing, God is not done with his plan to rescue his people from slavery.

45. "I will harden his heart"

» Exod. 4:21; see also 7:13, 22; 8:19; 9:12, 35; 10:20, 27; 11:10; 14:4, 8

Moses confronts Pharaoh and demands that he release the Hebrews from their bondage, at first simply for three days to worship God in the wilderness (chap. 44), but then permanently. Pharaoh refuses again and again, in spite of the plagues that God brings on the land of Egypt. Pharaoh is resolute in his decision not to let the Hebrews go. Why is he so incredibly stubborn?

The book of Exodus tells us that Pharaoh had a hard heart. In the Old Testament, "heart" often refers to a person's inner life and sometimes more specifically to the mind. A hard heart is one that is not malleable or changeable. A person who has a hard heart is stubborn even when the situation warrants a change of mind. But why is Pharaoh's heart so hard?

The answer to this question in Exodus disturbs many readers. Even before Moses returns to Egypt, God announces that, even though he will empower Moses to perform many miracles, "I will harden his [Pharaoh's] heart so he will refuse to let the people go" (Exod. 4:21; see also 7:3). After the plague of festering boils, "the Lord hardened Pharaoh's heart" (9:12). He hardens it after the plague of hail (10:1) and before the plague of locusts (10:20). He hardens it after the plague of darkness (10:27). He even hardens the king's heart after the announcement of the final plague, the death of the firstborn sons (11:10). Most climactically, God hardens Pharaoh's heart after he lets the Israelites go so that he pursues and attacks them at the sea (14:4, 8).

What does God want to accomplish by hardening Pharaoh's heart? The text is clear: Pharaoh's stubborn heart gives God the opportunity to glorify himself to this human being who thinks he is the most powerful person in the world and a god himself. His people believe this as well. Pharaoh's hard heart leads to the Lord heightening and intensifying the severity of the plagues that humiliate him and also the Egyptians who have humiliated God's people. God tells Moses that he will harden Pharaoh's heart "so I can multiply my miraculous signs and wonders in the land of Egypt. . . . When I raise my powerful hand and bring out the Israelites, the Egyptians will know that I am the LORD" (Exod. 7:3, 5). Then his hardening of Pharaoh's heart leads to the attack on the defenseless Israelites at the Red Sea. God says, "I have planned this in order to display my glory through Pharaoh and his whole army. After this the Egyptians will know that I am the LORD!" (14:4).

Still, it seems unfair, even unjust that Pharaoh and the Egyptians are punished if God makes him stubborn. But such a view misses the point. God did not make Pharaoh evil. Pharaoh was evil because of his own choices. Many passages make it clear that Pharaoh was responsible for his actions and for his own stubbornness. The narrator makes this point when he reports that Pharaoh hardened his own heart. After the plagues of frogs, flies, and hail the narrator reports that Pharaoh hardened his heart (Exod. 8:15, 32; 9:34).

God did not make Pharaoh evil or compel his evil choices; he just confirmed those choices and did not change his heart. Pharaoh and Egypt are responsible for the judgment that comes on them in the plagues. And God was indeed glorified and shown to be vastly superior to this arrogant human being.

46. "I will execute judgment against all the gods of Egypt, for I am the LORD!"

» Exod. 12:12

There is only one God. Or are there more?

On the eve of the final plague, the death of the firstborn throughout Egypt, God instructs the Israelites to commemorate their rescue by celebrating the first Passover (Exod. 12). On that night God will pass through the land of Egypt and "strike down every firstborn son and firstborn male animal." Then he proclaims, "I will execute judgment against all the gods of Egypt, for I am the LORD!" (12:12).

God not only brings judgment on Pharaoh and the Egyptian people but also on the Egyptian gods. Are we really to believe that the Egyptian gods are real? According to God in Exodus 12:12 they are.

When we think about the earlier story of the plagues, we can see that there are Egyptian gods, and these gods are a source of some power to the Egyptian wise men and magicians. When Aaron threw his staff down and it turned into a serpent, the Egyptians did the same (Exod. 7:10–13). This is not some kind of illusion; the Egyptians' staffs actually became serpents. However, even though the Egyptian wise men have some power from their gods, Yahweh's power is vastly superior, and that power is demonstrated when Aaron's serpent swallows up the Egyptians' serpents.

In the next episode, God turns the waters of the Nile into blood. The Egyptian wise men and magicians also turn some water into blood, demonstrating the power of their gods. However, as the plagues that follow intensify in severity, the Egyptian gods cannot keep pace with the God of the Israelites.

The Egyptian gods are real, but how does that align with the biblical teaching that there is only one God and he is Yahweh, the

God of Israel? Through Isaiah the prophet, for example, Yahweh proclaims this:

> I am the LORD;
> there is no other God.
> I have equipped you for battle,
> though you don't even know me,
> so all the world from east to west
> will know there is no other God.
> I am the LORD, and there is no other.
> I create the light and make the darkness.
> I send good times and bad times.
> I, the LORD, am the one who does these things.
>
> God is with you, and he is the only God.
> There is no other.
>
> For there is no other God but me,
> a righteous God and Savior.
> There is none but me. (Isa. 45:5–7, 14, 21)

How can there be only one God, Yahweh, but also Egyptian gods? The answer is that sometimes the Hebrews use the word G/god (*'elohim*) to refer to spiritual powers, powers created by God. More often Scripture calls these spiritual powers angels or demons. In the case of the Egyptian gods, since they oppress God's people and God fights them, they are the latter.

Once we understand the plagues as attacks on Egypt's gods, we can see how the Egyptians would have perceived them. Many, if not all, of the plagues were assaults on specific gods. Some are more obvious than others. For example, a god of fertility named Hapi was connected to the Nile River, which provided rich soil for planting when it annually flooded. Turning the Nile's water into blood was an assault on Hapi. In the next-to-last plague, the sun's light turns dark. The sun god went by various names—Amun,

Aten, Re—but by whatever name, he was one of Egypt's most important gods. When the sun's light was extinguished, the Egyptians would have seen this as an attack against the sun god. And the final plague, the death of the firstborn, including the firstborn of Pharaoh, was an attack on Pharaoh himself, who had godlike status among the Egyptians.

47. "I will erase the memory of Amalek from under heaven"

» Exod. 17:14; 17:8–16

See chapter 105.

EXODUS 19–24

God Makes a Covenant with Israel at Mount Sinai and Gives Them His Law

God had instructed Moses to lead Israel out of Egypt to the mountain where he had revealed himself from the burning bush (see chap. 42). Two months after departing Egypt, Moses brought the Israelites to Mount Sinai/Horeb. At this place, God entered into a covenant with Israel, with Moses acting as the mediator.

A covenant is similar to a treaty between the king of a great nation and a vassal (servant) people. God is like the king of a great nation, and Israel is like the vassal. God had previously entered into a covenant with Noah (Gen. 9) and then with Abraham (12:1–3; 15; 17). This new covenant, the Mosaic covenant, builds on these previous covenants and assures Israel that they are God's "special treasure" (Exod. 19:5). They will be a "kingdom of priests" (19:6) in that they will represent God to the rest of the nations. They were to bring God's blessing to all the families of the world (Gen. 12:3).

At Mount Sinai, God gives Israel what we today call the Ten Commandments (Exod. 20:1–17). God has saved them (20:2), and as a result, now they should obey him. God's gracious rescue of them comes before the obligation to show him obedience.

The Ten Commandments themselves are general theological/ethical demands. The first four concern Israel's relationship with God.

1. Yahweh must be their only God (20:3).
2. They must not construct an idol (20:4–6).
3. They must not misuse God's name (20:7).
4. They must observe the Sabbath (20:8–11).

The final six commandments concern relationships among the people.

5. They must honor their father and mother (20:12).
6. They must not murder (20:13).
7. They must not commit adultery (20:14).
8. They must not steal (20:15).
9. They must not bear false witness (20:16).
10. They must not covet (20:17).

A number of laws follow the Ten Commandments that are usually referred to as "case laws." These laws are closely related to and derive from the Ten Commandments. They apply the principles of the Ten Commandments to specific situations relevant to Israel in their particular cultural and redemptive-historical moment. In some cases, God does not demand his ideal but rather moves the people from where they are toward that ideal. We can recognize these cases as we compare the law to the creation account and observe the distance between the law and what we might call God's creation or Edenic ideal. In such cases, we can also see how the biblical law, though not the ideal, is closer than what we see in the surrounding cultures. We will illustrate this below as we examine some particularly difficult examples (see chaps. 52 and 57).

After the law, this section of Exodus ends with a ceremony that ratifies the covenant (Exod. 24). The people hear the law and say, "We will do everything the LORD has commanded" (24:3, 7). The remaining chapters of Exodus and the books that follow show how true to their word the Israelites turn out to be.

48. "You must not have any other god but me"

» Exod. 20:3

See chapter 86.

49. "You must not make for yourself an idol of any kind"

» Exod. 20:4; 20:4–6

See chapter 87.

50. "You must not misuse the name of the LORD your God"

» Exod. 20:7

See chapter 88.

51. "You must not covet"

» Exod. 20:17

See chapter 89.

52. "If you buy a Hebrew slave" and "If a man who has married a slave wife takes another wife for himself"

» Exod. 21:2, 10; 21:1–11

To most people in the twenty-first century, slavery is an unfathomable evil. Many readers today interpret Exodus 21:1–11 through the lens of the chattel slavery of the American past that brought millions of Africans to America, denying them freedom, tearing families apart, and subjecting people to sexual exploitation and physical abuse of the worst sort. We also know that slavery continues today in many countries, including illegally in the West. We might for good reasons expect the Bible to prohibit slavery of any kind, and we might be surprised and discouraged that, rather than rejecting slavery, the Old Testament allows it.

As mentioned in the introduction to this section of Scripture, the case laws are applications of the principles of the Ten Commandments to Israel at their cultural and redemptive-historical moment. This law of slavery applies the eighth commandment, "You must not steal" (Exod. 20:15). The law in Exodus 21 does not eradicate slavery, but it puts limits on having a slave that are unique to Israel in the ancient world. It's an example of taking people from where they are and moving them toward the creation ideal. The primary limit imposed on slavery in this law is a six-year term; the slave must be released in the seventh year (21:2). People became slaves during the Old Testament period for financial reasons. They were in debt, so they entered into the service of another person who would be required to care for them during their six years of service.

Debtors have six years to get their lives together. At the end of that time, the owner releases them and gives them resources to start life anew (Deut. 15:13–15). Thus, God regulates and uses the institution for good purposes. To keep a person in servitude longer than six years would break this law and the commandment that stands behind it. The "generous farewell gift" the master gives the departing slave helps the person get back on their feet (15:14).

In spite of the good purposes behind the law, the unfortunate reality is that sinful people abused it. The prophet Jeremiah tells us that during the reign of Zedekiah, the last king of Judah, the Babylonians were closing their net around Jerusalem (Jer. 34:1–7). Perhaps listening to Jeremiah's warning that their plight was due to their sin, including their abuse of slaves, the Israelites freed their slaves. Apparently, they had not been releasing them in the seventh year (34:8–22). Under pressure, they released the slaves. But only momentarily. They soon forced them back to labor, and God then announced that Babylon would indeed bring his judgment on them. God had taken his people where they were and moved them toward his creation ideal.

Reading Genesis 1–2 makes it impossible to imagine the institution of slavery being God's plan for humanity. We may then be surprised to turn to the New Testament and again see that God does not forbid slavery as such, but rather urges humane and even equal treatment of slaves (e.g., Gal. 3:28; Eph. 6:9; 1 Tim. 6:2; Philem. 1:16). However, these texts also must be read in their cultural context. Jesus and his followers were not in a place to eradicate slavery. Christians and the early church were themselves marginalized people. In spite of this marginalization, the New Testament provides theological principles that will lead later Christians to work for the abolition of slavery. As Paul says in his letter to the Galatians, "There is no longer Jew or Gentile, slave or free, male and female. For you are all one in Christ Jesus" (Gal. 3:28).

The same law that we have been looking at in Exodus 21 goes on to regulate but not prohibit polygamy, the taking of more than one wife. Condoning polygamy may be even more surprising than the allowance of slavery in the Old Testament case law.

In the figurative depiction of creation (see "Genesis 1–11: The Primeval History"), God forms woman because "it is not good for the man to be alone" (Gen. 2:18). Marriage is defined by God as a man leaving his parents and joining his wife such that "the two are united into one" (2:24). Two, not three or more, become one. Polygamy does not align with God's creation or Edenic ideal.

Still, in this case, God again takes people where they are and moves them toward the creation ideal. The case law in this situation protects the first wife from neglect and abuse by saying that the husband is obligated to give her "food, clothing, and sexual intimacy," and if he doesn't, she can leave him without making any payment (Exod. 21:10–11).

From this law in Exodus, we cannot argue that the Bible endorses polygamy. It doesn't, and polygamy was never God's ideal. In this case, however, we may be able to understand why God allowed it during the time of the Old Testament. For various reasons, in tribal societies like Israel's, women typically outnumbered men. Furthermore, single women, especially those without children, did not fare well. With many more women than men, polygamy may have been part of the solution at this particular historical period.

It's not clear what the status of polygamy is during the time of the New Testament. There is no explicit mention of it, and it was not widely practiced in the Greco-Roman world. Even so, polygamy was practiced in certain lands outside the Roman Empire. It is possible that one could have been a participant in good standing in a New Testament church and have had more than one wife. What is clear is that the officers of the church must be "the husband of one wife" (e.g., 1 Tim. 3:2, 12 ESV). This is a literal rendition of the Greek, and in my opinion, it means what it says, though some translations like the NLT will interpret it to mean that the officer must be "faithful to his wife." The point is that, even if one could be a member of a church, the officers needed to reflect God's creation ideal. As God's people, they should work to embody that ideal.

53. "Anyone who strikes father or mother must be put to death"

» Exod. 21:15

See chapter 100.

54. Anyone who dishonors father or mother must be put to death"

» Exod. 21:17

See chapter 100.

55. "She gives birth prematurely"

» Exod. 21:22; 21:22–25

This law is an application of the sixth commandment, "you must not murder" (Exod. 20:13). It concerns a situation where two men are fighting, and they hit a pregnant woman. The NLT (also the NIV) then presents the scenario that "she gives birth prematurely" (21:22). The NRSVue renders the Hebrew quite differently: "so that there is a miscarriage." The NLT/NIV translation says the fighting causes an early live birth, while the NRSVue asserts that the fetus comes out dead. All the major translations come out on one side or the other with the possible exception of the ESV, which translates "so that her children come out" with no explicit indicator of whether the children are dead or alive (though it is likely that the translators would apply "there is no harm" to the children and the mother). How can there be such a difference and what are the implications for the different translations?

Comparing Four English Translations of Exodus 21:22

ESV	"When men strive together and hit a pregnant woman, **so that her children come out**, but there is no harm, the one who hit her shall surely be fined, as the woman's husband shall impose on him, and he shall pay as the judges determine."
NIV	"If people are fighting and hit a pregnant woman and **she gives birth prematurely** but there is no serious injury, the offender must be fined whatever the woman's husband demands and the court allows."
NLT	"Now suppose two men are fighting, and in the process they accidentally strike a pregnant woman **so she gives birth prematurely**. If no further injury results, the man who struck the woman must pay the amount of compensation the woman's husband demands and the judges approve."
NRSVue	"When people who are fighting injure a pregnant woman **so that there is a miscarriage** and yet no further harm follows, the one responsible shall be fined what the woman's husband demands, paying as much as the judges determine."

Turning to the Hebrew, we can note the ambiguity that modern translators face. The Hebrew simply says, "her children come out." It does not explicitly say whether they are dead or alive. Both the NLT and the NRSVue are providing their considered interpretation to clarify the situation, which is perfectly appropriate in terms of translation theory. That the NLT knows that the NRSVue translation is a possible one is seen by the footnote that gives the alternative rendering. (When a translation provides an alternative rendering such as this, it indicates that the translators were divided and acknowledge the Hebrew might support the alternate rendering.)

Unfortunately, we can't be dogmatic about the translation, but there are good reasons to prefer the NRSVue translation that the altercation resulted in a miscarriage, not a live birth. First, the verb that is used ("to come out") appears also in Numbers

12:12 in a context that refers to a miscarriage. Second, in the ancient world before the advent of modern medicine, a premature birth almost always ended in death, so if the child "came out" the presumption would be that the result was a miscarriage. Also significant is how the early Greek translation, the Septuagint, renders the Hebrew:

> If two men fight and they strike a woman who is pregnant, and her child comes but while not yet fully formed, he will be forced to pay a fine; whatever the woman's husband imposes, he will pay with a valuation. But if it is fully formed, he will give life for life, eye for eye, tooth for tooth, hand for hand, foot for foot, burning for burning, wound for wound, stripe for stripe. (Exod. 21:22–24 NETS)

The Septuagint makes clear that these early Jewish translators believed the Hebrew indicated a miscarriage. Like modern versions, the Septuagint offers an interpretation. It is not infallible. But the significance of the Septuagint is that it was the Bible of Jesus's day and also of the early church. By that time Hebrew was primarily a literary language that only scholars could read, so most Jews and Christians used the Septuagint. Accordingly, the Septuagint rendition gives us a window into how the text was understood then.

Why all the concern about the translation? What is the difference in terms of what the law is saying?

In the school of thought represented by the NLT and NIV, if there is harm done that results in a premature birth (but not death) of the fetus and no serious injury to the woman or the child, then there is a monetary fine. But if there is "serious injury" to the woman or the child, then there is to be an equivalent penalty to the person or persons who caused the harm.

In the school of thought represented by the NRSVue, the monetary fine applies to the miscarriage. In the Septuagint rendition, there is a gradation of moral violation so that if it is early in the pregnancy and the fetus is not yet fully formed, then there is a fine, but beyond that there is a more serious culpability. This view also believes that the *lex talionis* ("eye for an eye," chap. 56) applies only to the woman.

56. "An eye for an eye"

» Exod. 21:24; 21:23–25

Three times in the Torah, the law lays down a principle of punishment that is known today by the Latin term *lex talionis*, which roughly means "law of retaliation" or "retribution" (Exod. 21:23–25; Lev. 24:19–20; Deut. 19:21). The principle is that "the punishment must match the injury" (Exod. 21:23). The examples that follow trouble modern readers: "an eye for an eye, a tooth for a tooth, a hand for a hand, a foot for a foot, a burn for a burn, a wound for a wound, a bruise for a bruise" (21:24–25). Does this law mean that causing physical harm always results in the equivalent physical harm of the perpetrator? If someone blinds another person, does that mean that the criminal is then blinded? If someone knocks out the teeth of a person, are his or her teeth also knocked out?

Apparently not. The next law actually addresses the situation where a person hits a slave and either blinds them or knocks out their teeth (Exod. 21:26–27). The stated punishment is not a literal equivalence; rather, the person must "let the slave go free to compensate" for the eye or the tooth.

Lex talionis may sound like ancient Israel would have a number of physical punishments that would involve dismemberment and the like, but they did not (see chap. 57 for the death penalty). One exception is in Deuteronomy 25:11–12. In this passage, a woman breaks up a fight between her husband and another man by grabbing the latter by his testicles. To punish the woman, "you must cut off her hand." This is indeed a difficult text but is notably unique in its call for some form of mutilation. The rarity of such a punishment contrasts with the broader ancient Near Eastern law collections, like the Code of Hammurabi, which calls for mutilation as the punishment for a number of crimes.

That said, the principle expressed by *lex talionis* is quite humane when judged by potential alternatives. The law calls for punishment that is equivalent to the crime. This principle guards against the sinful human desire to hurt someone even more than we have been hurt. In its ancient setting, *lex talionis* guards against the excessive retribution so disturbingly expressed by Lamech in the early chapters of Genesis:

> Adah and Zillah, hear my voice;
> listen to me, you wives of Lamech.
> I have killed a man who attacked me,
> a young man who wounded me.
> If someone who kills Cain is punished seven times,
> then the one who kills me will be punished seventy-seven times! (Gen. 4:23–24)

In the final analysis, the principle of equivalent punishment expressed by *lex talionis* is not only humane but is also the foundation for modern legal theory in America and beyond.

Jesus refers to *lex talionis* in the Sermon on the Mount (Matt. 5:38–42). He tells his audience that they have heard the "punishment must match the injury." He goes on to suggest that rather than seeking punishment, his followers should make themselves vulnerable to more injury. For instance, "If someone slaps you on the right cheek, offer the other cheek also" (5:39). Jesus is wrongly heard if he is taken to mean there should be no punishments for crimes on civic or national levels. Rather, he is talking about relatively minor personal injuries and insults that his followers should be willing to bear without recourse to the courts.

57. "Must be put to death"

» Exod. 21:15; many places in the law

The laws that follow the Ten Commandments, the case laws, apply the principles of the Ten to specific situations according to the cultural and redemptive-historical moment of the people of God during the Old Testament period (see the introduction to Exod. 19–24). Besides the laws themselves, readers today wonder how to think about the penalties associated with these laws, particularly the pronouncement of the death penalty.

The list of crimes that call for the death penalty includes murder (Exod. 21:14), attacking or cursing a father or a mother (21:15, 17), kidnapping (21:16), owning a bull that gores people to death (21:29), bestiality (22:19), desecrating the Sabbath (31:14), sacrificing a child to a false god (Lev. 20:4), committing adultery (20:10), engaging in same-sex sexual relations (20:13), and more.

What are we to make of these penalties? How did they function during the Old Testament time period? Should they inform our legal system today?

Knowing how the death penalty functioned in ancient Israel is not as straightforward as one might think. There are reasons to doubt that Israelite courts applied these penalties. First, the historical books include accounts of people who break these laws but do not receive the death penalty. Probably best known is the story of David and Bathsheba (2 Sam. 11). David commits adultery. He also has Uriah killed. Nathan confronts David (2 Sam. 12). He repents, but there is no hint of the idea that he should be put to death.

Second, for most of these crimes, the death penalty seems to be the maximum but not the only possible penalty. Numbers 35:31 says, "You must never accept a ransom payment for the life of someone judged guilty of murder and subject to execution; murderers must always be put to death." This statement strongly implies that a lesser penalty could be applied in all other offenses except murder. This is explicit in the law concerning the goring ox, which says, "The dead person's relatives may accept payment to compensate for the loss of life. The owner of the ox may redeem his life paying whatever is demanded" (Exod. 21:30).

Finally, considering the law in the light of ancient Near Eastern law collections, we have reason to believe that they and their penalties were not necessarily used by courts. Rather, they are the expression of ethical ideals. We have records of actual court cases, and they are not guided by the law collections or their associated penalties.

But what about today? Why don't Christians advocate for the death penalty for all the crimes listed above and more? Unfortunately, some Christians do exactly that. Theonomists (also called Christian Reconstructionists) believe that American society should be ordered by the Old Testament law, including its penalties. But this is a serious and dangerous hermeneutical error.

The hermeneutical error is not recognizing that, while there is continuity between the Old Testament and the New Testament, there is also discontinuity. In this case, the discontinuity is that God's people during the Old Testament time were a nation-state (Israel), while in the New Testament period, the people of God are the church, drawn from many different nations. We are a spiritual entity, not a political one.

As a spiritual entity, the church does not exercise physical punishment. Ancient Israel was to be holy to reflect its holy God. Such holiness was to attract others to God. Now that Jesus has come, it is the church that should reflect God's holiness. Of course, Christians sin, and when they do, they must repent. In the case of egregious unrepented sin, there is a spiritual punishment, namely excommunication. Paul calls for the excommunication ("you should remove this man from your fellowship," 1 Cor. 5:2) of a man who is sleeping with his father's wife. Paul says that this excommunication is necessary not only for the church but for the man, so "his sinful nature will be destroyed and he himself will be saved on the day the Lord returns" (5:5).

58. "You must not cook a young goat in its mother's milk"

» Exod. 23:19

The last case law that follows the Ten Commandments in the book of Exodus strikes modern readers as strange and difficult to explain. Case laws apply the principles of the Ten Commandments to specific situations according to the cultural and redemptive-historical moment of the people of God during the Old Testament time period (see the introduction to Exod. 19–24). But it is impossible to be certain about the principle behind the prohibition of cooking a young goat in its mother's milk, though we have some intriguing possible solutions.

Some case laws keep Israelites from engaging in Canaanite religious practices. For instance, when the altar law (Exod. 20:22–26) prohibits building steps leading up the altar, it does so because if the priest goes up steps, then "someone might look up under your clothing and see your nakedness" (20:26). While this prohibition may strike a modern reader as somewhat humorous and concerned about a personal violation, the real reason behind this law almost certainly has to do with sexual rituals that were practiced by the Canaanites. Worship of Yahweh will have nothing like that associated with it.

That cooking a young goat in its mother's milk might be a religious practice would be supported by the context, since the laws concerning three annual religious festivals precede this law (Exod. 23:14–19a). Some have thought that cooking a young goat in its mother's milk reflects Canaanite religion, based on an ancient Near Eastern text that seems to refer to the practice. However, the text is broken and hard to read so unfortunately does not provide strong support for the idea.

Today some believe that the rationale for the law is obvious in that it is inherently repulsive to think of a baby goat stewing in its own mother's milk. In the final analysis, we just can't be certain, and in any case, there is no reason to think that the law applies to Christians today. In Jewish circles, the law plays a very significant role in keeping kosher. Conservative Jews will never mix meat and dairy products in any way, so they can never be guilty of breaking this law.

EXODUS 25–40

Building the Tabernacle

The book of Exodus has three major parts. The first describes how God rescued Israel from Egyptian bondage (Exod. 1–18), and the second narrates how God gives Israel the law (Exod. 19–24). In the third and final section (Exod. 25–40), God instructs Moses how to build the tabernacle.

This third section of Exodus has three parts. In Exodus 25–31, God instructs Moses on building the tabernacle and the furniture (bronze altar, incense altar, lampstand, ark of the covenant, table of presence) that goes with it. The final chapters (Exod. 35–40) narrate the actual construction of the tabernacle. There is a lot of repetition between the first and the third parts to demonstrate how Israel followed God's instructions down to the letter. The main difference between these two sections is the verbs. In the instructions, God speaks in the imperative mood, giving commands, while in the third part, the verbs are rendered in English as past tense (for the Hebrew perfect aspect). For example, in Exodus 25:10 God says to Moses, "Have the people make an Ark of acacia wood—a sacred chest 45 inches long, 27 inches wide, and 27 inches high." Then in Exodus 37:1 we read, "Bezalel made the Ark of acacia wood—a sacred chest 45 inches long, 27 inches wide, and 27 inches high."

The purpose of the repetition in these two sections is to demonstrate that Israel followed God's instructions exactly. This message is particularly important because the middle section (Exod. 32–34) tells the story of the golden calf, where the Israelites undertake an unauthorized and false form of worship. While Moses is on Mount Sinai receiving the commandments and instructions, the people grow impatient and ask Aaron, the high priest, to make them "some gods who can lead us" (32:1). Aaron obliges by fashioning a golden calf and presenting it as "the gods who brought you out of the land of Egypt" (32:4). It's hard to believe that the people whom God rescued from Egypt could so quickly turn against him in this way, but they did (see chap. 64).

When Moses returns from the mountain, he is angry at their false worship and throws down the stone tablets with God's instructions, breaking them. Since the tablets represent God's special relationship with his people, breaking them signifies a break in that relationship. The Israelites have broken the covenant, and God is so angry that he tells Moses he will destroy them and start anew. Moses, however, intercedes with God so that he "changed his mind about the terrible disaster he had threatened to bring on his people" (Exod. 32:14).

Moses confronts Aaron and then calls for "all of you who are on the LORD's side, come here and join me" (Exod. 32:26). His fellow Levites respond to this call, and they kill about three thousand calf worshipers. For their obedience, Moses ordains the Levites to priestly duty (see chap. 64).

Though God had already decided not to destroy Israel completely for their horrible sin (Exod. 32:14), he was still determined to judge them by bringing a plague on them (32:35). He also decided to remove his immediate presence from them. Even so, he reveals himself personally to Moses, who stands in a crevice of a cliff wall (33:19–23). God also presents Moses with a new copy of the law.

The first and third parts of this final section of Exodus are lengthy descriptions of the tabernacle. The tabernacle is a tent, but a tent of royal magnificence. In Numbers 2, we learn that God's tent is to be erected in the center of the camp, the place where the king's tent was located when his army was on the march.

The description of the innermost curtain covering the tabernacle is such that the tabernacle as a whole represents heaven on earth, while the three additional coverings over the innermost one are essentially weatherproofing (see chap. 61). The distribution of metals in the tabernacle moves from bronze to silver to gold to pure gold as one moves from the outer courtyard into the Holy Place within the tent and finally into the innermost Most Holy Place (where the ark of the covenant is located). Later Scripture calls the ark God's footstool. In other words, God, the king, was enthroned in the Most Holy Place. In the Holy Place, the tree symbolism of the lampstand, or menorah, indicated to the Israelites that the tabernacle was not only heaven on earth but also a reminder of Eden (see chap. 60).

God initiated the building of the tabernacle. Neither Moses nor the Israelites came up with the idea; God commanded its construction (Exod. 25:8). He also provided all the materials for its construction. True, the people donated the materials (25:1–7), but they only had these things because God induced the Egyptians to give them to the Israelites as they left Egypt (12:34–36). Further, God gave the plans to Moses, requiring them to build "according to the pattern I will show you" (25:9; cf. 25:40; 26:30; 27:8). God even gave the skill to the builders to construct the tabernacle. Of the chief craftsman, Bezalel, God says, "I have filled him with the Spirit of God, giving him great wisdom, ability, and expertise in all kinds of crafts" (31:4). God says the same about Oholiab, his assistant, as well as all the others who will work on the structure (31:6).

59. "Have the people make an Ark"

» Exod. 25:10; 25:10–22

The ark of the covenant is the most potent symbol of God's presence in the Old Testament. It is the piece of furniture that is in the Most Holy Place. Elsewhere it is called God's footstool (1 Chron. 28:2; Pss. 99:5; 132:7)—that is, the footstool of God's throne. God was imagined to be enthroned above it. The ark was also mobile, able to be transported by priests using poles attached by rings. In this way, they could carry the ark through the wilderness and also later into battles.

When the ark was first built, the stone tablets containing the commandments were placed in it. Later, some manna was placed inside the ark, and Aaron's budding staff was laid in front of it (16:33–34; Num. 17:10, see chap. 82).

60. "Make a lampstand of pure, hammered gold"

» Exod. 25:31; 25:31–40

While the tabernacle's innermost curtain indicates that the structure, as a whole, symbolized heaven on earth (see chap. 61), the lampstand or menorah reminded people of the garden of Eden (Exod. 25:31–40). The description of this golden lampstand uses a lot of arboreal language. The lamp has six branches from a center stem. These branches will have "cups shaped like almond blossoms, complete with buds and petals" (25:33–34).

Thus, the lampstand is a tree in a place where God makes his special presence known. God makes his presence known among his people as he did to Adam and Eve in the garden of Eden where there was the tree of life. The lampstand is specifically an almond tree, though there is no indication that the tree in the garden was of the almond variety. But then in Numbers 17 when God wants to affirm Aaron's and the Levites' special role among the tribes,

God causes Aaron's staff not only to sprout, bud, and blossom, but also to produce "ripe almonds" (Num. 17:8; see chap. 82).

61. "Make the Tabernacle from ten curtains of finely woven linen"

» Exod. 26:1; 26:1–14

The tabernacle is a tent. It is God's tent and therefore quite ornate since it is the tent of the king. A tent is an appropriate form for God's dwelling on earth during the period from Moses to Solomon. God's people are not yet settled in the land and won't be completely so until David finally subdues all the internal enemies of Israel. Before the people enter the promised land, God tells Moses that it will not be until God "gives you rest from all your enemies and you're living safely in the land" that he will choose a place to make his presence known (Deut. 12:10–11). This happens with David, allowing his son Solomon to build the temple, an immovable home for God. Until then, a tent that can be packed up and moved is appropriate for the place where God makes his presence known among the Israelites.

Like any tent, God's has coverings (Exod. 26:1–14). The sides and back of the tent were acacia wood panels and the front was open. Thus, the first or innermost covering or curtain was the inside roof of the tent and would be seen by those priests who went into the tent (26:1–6). This curtain was made by taking ten curtains of finely woven linen and combining them, attaching them with golden clasps. These curtains were made of "blue, purple, and scarlet thread and with skillfully embroidered cherubim" (26:1).

This description indicates that the tabernacle represents heaven on earth. The deep blue of the linen with cherubim woven into it turns this earthly place into a microcosm of heaven. Cherubim are the most powerful of God's angelic beings. They serve as his bodyguards and are the nearest to him among the angels.

This precious and significant curtain was itself topped by three others. The first was one of "goat-hair cloth" (Exod. 26:7). On top of this one they placed two others, one of "tanned ram skins" and another of "fine goatskin leather" (26:14). These each attached eleven rather than ten parts together to make them larger than the first one. The additional length allowed them to completely cover the innermost curtain. They functioned as weatherproofing, keeping that very precious and expensive innermost curtain away from the elements. These parts were connected by brass rather than gold clasps, signifying importance but not as important or immediately exposed to the interior as the innermost curtain.

62. The incense altar, the table, and the bronze altar

» Exod. 30:1–10; 25:23–30; 27:1–8

While the ark, lampstand, and curtain may be the most interesting and revealing of the symbolism of the tabernacle as the place where God made his presence known, other pieces of furniture served important purposes and were counterparts to objects found in the Israelites' tents.

Inside the tabernacle in the Holy Place was an incense altar (Exod. 30:1–10). From this altar sweet smells wafted through the tabernacle. It was small—eighteen inches square and three feet tall. It was made of acacia wood and covered in pure gold since it was close to the Most Holy Place. The ornate incense altar in the tabernacle has its counterpart in small portable incense burners that archaeologists have found in the remains of ancient Israelite houses.

Also inside the tabernacle was a table—three feet long, 18 inches wide, and 27 inches high (Exod. 25:23–30). Positioned close to the ark and the presence of God, the table also was covered with pure gold. Like a table in an Israelite home, this one had bread on it—twelve loaves representing the twelve tribes

(Lev. 24:5–9). The priests placed fresh bread out every Sabbath, and only they were allowed to eat it.

The final piece of furniture mentioned was the altar on which sacrifices were offered (Exod. 27:1–8). Standing in the courtyard of the tabernacle and so farther from the Most Holy Place, the altar was made of acacia wood covered with bronze. It had a horn or protrusion at each of the four corners, which may have helped with tying down a sacrifice, but this is far from certain. This altar also had a counterpart in the oven that would have been placed outside a typical Israelite tent.

Thus, the tabernacle represented God's presence among his people. He, like them, lived in a tent, but a special tent fit for a king.

63. "Insert the Urim and Thummim into the sacred chestpiece"

» Exod. 28:30

Exodus 28 describes the manufacture of priestly clothing. In this context the Urim and Thummim appear (Exod. 28:30). These objects have generated much fascination because they seem to function like divination, which Scripture prohibits (Deut. 18:9–14). Indeed, God tells Moses that the high priest should place the Urim and Thummim in the sacred chestpiece worn over the ephod (Exod. 28:29: Lev. 8:8); "so they will be carried over Aaron's heart when he goes into the LORD's presence. In this way, Aaron will always carry over his heart the objects used to determine the LORD's will of this people whenever he goes in before the LORD" (Exod. 28:30).

The Urim and Thummim were objects that the high priest used to discover the will of God in particular situations. An example comes from 1 Samuel 23:1–6, where David inquires of God whether he should do battle against the Philistines who were plundering the city of Keilah. The passage does not explicitly mention the Urim and Thummim, but David puts questions before the Lord, and the Lord answers him. At the end of the episode, almost like a parenthetical expression, we read, "When Abiathar son of Ahimelech fled to David at Keilah, he brought the ephod with him" (23:6). One might wonder why the narrator provides this information, and the only reason would be to inform them how David made his inquiry. Abiathar was high priest, so he had the Urim and Thummim with him. Interestingly, the narrator says Abiathar brought the ephod with him. Exodus 28 and Leviticus 8 say that the high priest carried the Urim and Thummim in his chestpiece, but the ephod and the chestpiece were connected. Some interpreters think that the ephod also covered the upper body of the priest (though others believe the ephod was like an apron).

Moses's blessing of the Levite tribe includes the Urim and Thummim: "O Lord, you have given your Thummim and Urim—the sacred lots—to your faithful servants the Levites" (Deut. 33:8). The overall commendation of this priestly tribe is in their role of guarding the covenant (33:9)—namely, the relationship between God and his people. The Urim and Thummim help to keep the relationship strong by revealing God's will to Israel in specific situations.

It is highly likely that when the biblical text refers to "lots," it most often means the Urim and Thummim. Certainly that is the case when the high priest throws lots to determine God's will and make a decision, such as when God distributes land to the various tribes (Josh. 14:2; 18:6, 8). These lots are said to be "cast" or "thrown" (Lev. 16:8), which hints at how they were used. It is likely that a question would be posed, the lots (Urim and Thummim) would be cast, and an answer would be given (or not; see next paragraph). The lots would either be affirmative or negative, and in this way God would give direction to Israel.

However, sometimes God chose not to answer even when the sacred lots were cast. We learn this from a story on the eve of Saul's death. God had earlier deserted Saul because of his disobedience. As he fought the Philistines, Saul sought God's will: "He asked the LORD what to do, but the LORD refused to answer him, either by dreams or by sacred lots or by prophets" (1 Sam. 28:6). This episode makes it clear that the lots could be cast after asking a question, but the result in Saul's case was silence, with no answer to the question. Perhaps (and this is speculative) the Urim and Thummim were two dice, and both had to come up yes or no for a positive or negative answer. If they split, then there was no answer.

In this way, the Urim and Thummim could not force a response from God. God is free to answer or not. This makes the Urim and Thummim different from the divination condemned by Deuteronomy 18. In other forms of divination, such as reading a sheep's liver, pouring oil into water, or astrology, there is always an answer, but not so with the Urim and Thummim.

Finally, we conclude by commenting on the probable meaning of the words *Urim* and *Thummim*. Urim is related to the Hebrew term for "light" and Thummim to the word for "truth." Casting the Urim and Thummim brings God's light and truth.

64. "Today you have ordained yourselves for the service of the LORD"

» Exod. 32:29; 32:1–30

How did the Levites get their priestly jobs? The answer to that question is in the story of the golden calf. The last part of the book of Exodus (Exod. 25–40) concerns the building of the tabernacle. God gives instructions to build the tabernacle in Exodus 25–31, and the narrator describes the actual building of the structure in Exodus 35–40. The chapters between these two sections tell the story of a grave threat to proper worship.

While Moses is on Mount Sinai receiving the commandments and instructions, the people grow impatient and ask Aaron, the high priest, to make them "some gods [*'elohim*] who can lead us" (32:1). Aaron obliges by fashioning a golden calf and presenting it as "the gods [*'elohim*] who brought you out of the land of Egypt" (32:4). It's a little unclear exactly what the golden calf represents. Part of the issue is that the term translated "gods" (*'elohim*), while plural, often is used as a singular to refer to Yahweh, the true God of Israel. After constructing the golden calf, Aaron announces, "Tomorrow will be a festival to the LORD [Yahweh]" (Exod. 32:5). Whether the golden calf represents false gods or Yahweh himself, it is an idol and the people's worship of it is a false form of worship since the second commandment prohibits the making of idols, even of Yahweh himself (20:4–6).

On the mountain, God tells Moses what has happened below and his intention to destroy the people in his anger. He informs Moses that once he destroys them he will make Moses into a great nation (Exod. 32:10), in essence starting over by making him the new Abraham. In response, Moses intercedes with God so that God does not destroy the people. He succeeds, though punishment will still come on the idol worshipers.

As Moses descends from the mountain he breaks the two tablets of the covenant law, symbolizing the break in the relationship between God and Israel caused by the people's covenant infidelity. Moses then takes the calf idol and burns it, grinds it to powder, scatters the powder into water, and makes the Israelites drink it.

Moses confronts Aaron, who makes the excuse that the people pressured him and all he did was gather the gold jewelry, throw it into the fire, and the calf, as if by magic, just emerged from the fire. In spite of Aaron's weak defense, Moses's anger focuses on those who worshiped the calf. He calls those who are on the Lord's side to come to him, and the Levites respond.

He then instructs the Levites to get swords and go among the calf worshipers to kill them. They obey and kill about three thousand people. For their work as God's agents of judgment,

Moses announces, "Today you have ordained yourselves for the service of the Lord, for you obeyed him even though it meant killing your own sons and brothers" (Exod. 32:29). On that day they were consecrated for special priestly duty.

We might ask why their actions led to their ordination as priests. The answer is obvious once we understand that priests are guardians of God's holiness. At the end of his life, Moses describes the Levites and their priestly responsibilities as guarding the covenant, even as he remembers what they did to the calf worshipers (Deut. 33:8–11). Most priestly guarding of the covenant is preemptive. Priests teach the law so that God's people might know how to obey him. They offer sacrifices when the people break the law in order to restore Israel's relationship with God. Serving as doorkeepers, they guard the sacred precinct of the tabernacle and later the temple.

Note the significance that it was the Levites who responded to Moses's call and thus were granted this special priestly role. Remember that Levi, the father figure of the tribe, along with his brother Simeon drew the anger of their father Jacob because of their actions at Shechem (see chap. 34). Their actions led Jacob to curse them at the end of his life, saying their descendants would be scattered throughout the land when Israel took possession of it; they would not receive a tribal allotment (see chap. 39). With his words, Jacob intended that the tribes descending from these men would lose their tribal distinctiveness, but this did not happen to the Levites. They were indeed scattered and given cities within the boundaries of other tribes (Josh. 21), but because of their actions against the calf worshipers, they became the most distinctive of all the tribes because of their priestly status.

LEVITICUS 1-7

Making Offerings to the Lord

The Torah's five books are a single literary composition. Leviticus is part 3 of this piece of writing. Its first seven chapters pause the narrative storyline as God gives Moses instructions for five different types of offerings: the burnt offering (*'olah*), the grain offering (*minhah*), the peace offering (*shelamim*), the sin offering (*hatta't*), and the guilt offering (*'asham*). These five offerings illustrate how Israel might seek atonement, make a gift to God, and enjoy fellowship in God's presence. The following chapters will examine each of these offerings and focus on issues that are difficult for the modern reader to understand. The action of the narrative that began in Genesis picks up again in Leviticus 8–10 with the ordination of the priests, followed by the story of the ritual violations of Aaron's sons Nadab and Abihu.

65. "If the animal you present as a burnt offering [*'olah*]"

» Lev. 1:3; 1:3–17; 6:8–13

The first offering in Leviticus 1–7 is an *'olah* in Hebrew. The word is from a verb meaning "to rise" or "to go up" and likely references the smoke that ascends heavenward as the offering is made. English versions typically render the word as "burnt offering" or "whole burnt offering" since what makes it distinctive is that the whole animal is burned on the altar.

The burnt offering can be a bull, a sheep, or a bird. The animal must be male and have no blemish. The offerer places his hands on the head of the animal in a ritual of identification. The animal now represents the worshiper. The animal is then slaughtered, and the blood is splashed around the altar. Finally, the animal is placed on the altar and completely burned.

The purpose of this offering is to make atonement with God. Sin has broken a person's relationship with God and deserves punishment. The animal suffers the punishment that the offerer deserved, and thus the person can be reconciled with God. Atonement has been accomplished; God and the person are "at one" again. The NLT captures the meaning of atonement when it translates the relevant verb (*kipper*) as "making right" between God and the worshiper (Lev. 1:4).

Leviticus 1 gives instructions for a burnt offering of an animal from the herd (Lev. 1:3–9), an animal from a flock (1:10–13), or a bird (1:14–17). Whether one offers a bull, a sheep, or a bird depends on their wherewithal, a bull being very expensive, a sheep less so, and one might even trap a bird for free. Not everyone can afford a bull or sheep, but that should not prohibit a person from repenting and seeking reconciliation with God.

66. "When you present grain [*minhah*]"

» Lev. 2:1; 2:1–16; 6:14–23

The grain offering (*minhah*) is next. The Hebrew word means "gift" or "tribute," the type of gift made to a king—in this case, the divine king. The offering's name announces its purpose: to give a gift to God. Most English translations render *minhah* as "grain offering" since grain is the primary component.

This offering can come cooked or uncooked. Its basic configuration involves choice flour, olive oil, and a bit of frankincense.

The priest takes some of the flour and oil with all of the frankincense and burns it on the altar. The frankincense results in a pleasant smell. The bulk of the grain offering is then given to the priests, presumably so that they and their families could eat it.

The most interesting feature of this offering is the command never to add yeast or honey to the offering and always to add salt (Lev. 2:11, 13). The ancient audience would know the significance of these demands, but the text doesn't explain. We can only make an educated guess. The Hebrew word for honey here means fruit honey. When burned, both yeast and honey ferment, which is a form of decay. That may explain the prohibition. As for salt, the text does connect the *minhah* with the "eternal covenant" (2:13). Apparently, something about salt symbolizes the eternality of the covenant. Interestingly, nothing happens when salt is burned with fire. So, speculating, it may be that the salt survives the fire just as the covenant survives trouble and even rebellion.

67. "If you present an animal from the herd as a peace offering [*shelamim*]"

» Lev. 3:1; 3:1–17; 7:11–21

The peace offering is described in Leviticus 3. The translation "peace offering" reflects well the Hebrew *shelamim*, which has the root connected to the well-known Hebrew word *shalom*, meaning peace. Other translations render the word "fellowship offering" (NIV), and this translation expresses the offering's main function.

There may be some atonement value to this offering since the offerer lays hands on the animal, slaughters it, and then splashes the blood on the altar similar to the burnt offering. But for this offering, only "all the fat around the internal organs, the two kidneys and the fat around them near the loins, and the long lobe of the liver" are removed and burned as a gift to God (Lev. 3:3–5). The rest of the animal is cooked and enjoyed by the worshipers.

This sacrifice carries a prohibition that God's people "never eat any fat or blood" (3:17; cf. Lev. 17). Since the blood represents life, this prohibition assures that the animal will be dead (17:11, 14; Deut. 12:23). Perhaps the same can be said about the fat.

68. "He must give a sin offering [*hatta't*]"

» Lev. 4:3; 4:1–5:13; 6:24–30

The names of both the sin offering (*hatta't*) and the guilt offering (*'asham*; see chap. 69) indicate these are atonement sacrifices like the burnt offering in Leviticus 1. As with the burnt offering, for these offerings the worshiper lays hands on the animal and slaughters it. With his finger, the high priest then sprinkles some of the blood in front of the inner curtain of the sanctuary and puts some of it on the horns of the incense altar. The priest then pours the rest of the blood at the base of the outside sacrificial altar. The fat and some of the internal organs are burned on the altar, and then the rest of the animal is burned outside the camp.

The type of animal offered for the sin offering depends on who offers it. If the high priest is bringing an offering for his own sin, then he must offer a young bull (Lev. 4:3–12). If it is the entire Israelite community, then they too must bring a young bull (4:13–21). If the worshiper is a nonpriestly leader of the community, then he must bring a male goat (4:22–26). If it is "any of the common people" (4:27), then they can bring a female goat or a female sheep (4:27–35). The more important (or numerous, in the case of the entire community) the offerer, the more expensive the offering. This gradation reflects the damage that can be done to the community by a leader.

The sin offering is given when someone commits a sin unknowingly but then becomes aware of it later on. Leviticus 5:1–6 presents several scenarios where a sin offering is appropriate (refusing to testify in court, touching something ceremonially unclean, taking a foolish vow). Leviticus 5:7–13 allows for alternative offerings (two turtledoves or two pigeons or two quarts of choice flour) if a person cannot afford an animal like a goat or a bull.

69. "You must bring a guilt offering [*'asham*]"

» Lev. 5:15; 5:14–6:7; 7:1–10

The guilt offering directions appear in Leviticus 5–7. A guilt offering is required when an offense incurs some kind of financial loss. Here the animal to be sacrificed "must be slaughtered at the place where the burnt offerings are slaughtered, and its blood must be splattered against the sides of the altar" (7:2). After splashing the blood against the altar, the priest burns some of the internal organs and the fat. The rest of the animal is given to the priest, who may eat it along with any other males in his family.

The unique feature of a guilt offering is the restitution required. This is because people offered guilt offerings when their actions caused another person financial loss. That loss must be repaid along with a 20 percent fine (Lev. 6:5).

LEVITICUS 8-10

The Priests Begin Their Work

Leviticus 8 recounts the ordination of the priests, in particular Aaron and his sons. The service, led by Moses, took place at the entrance to the tabernacle. Moses began by washing the priests with water, likely signifying their cleansing as they move from the realm of the ordinary to the holy. He then dressed Aaron in his high priestly garments (see Exod. 28). The priestly garments included an ornate robe, the ephod, a decorative sash, a chest-piece in which was placed the Urim and Thummim (see chap. 63), and a turban with a gold medallion placed in the front of it. Some materials of the priestly clothing reflected the material used in the tabernacle itself. The priests became holy, or set apart, in order to serve in a holy place.

Next Moses took oil and anointed the tabernacle and all its utensils. He then poured oil on the head of Aaron (see Ps. 133). This ritual consecrated the holy place and also set apart the high priest as holy and a part of the tabernacle. Priests were servants of God in his royal residence.

Moses then began a series of sacrifices, beginning with a bull for a sin offering. Aaron and his sons laid their hands on it, but interestingly this sacrifice purifies, or makes atonement, for the altar itself (Lev. 8:15). Second, Moses presented a ram as a burnt offering (8:18–21). Aaron and his sons again laid their hands on it and offered it as a gift to God. A second ram was used as an ordination offering (8:22–24). Moses applied the blood of this animal to the right ear, right thumb, and right big toe of Aaron and his sons. Moses then took parts of the ram and placed on top of them "a thin cake of bread made without yeast, a cake of bread mixed with olive oil, and a wafer spread with olive oil" (8:26). Aaron lifted this offering up to God, and then Moses burned it all.

Moses took some of the anointing oil and blood and sprinkled them on Aaron and his sons, as well as on their clothing. "In this way, he made Aaron and his sons and their garments holy" (Lev. 8:30).

Finally, Aaron and his sons ate some of the meat of the offerings along with some bread. Moses instructed them to stay at the entrance of the tabernacle for seven days. After this, the ordination would be complete. Moses warned Aaron and his sons that they must be very careful to follow God's instructions in detail because "if you fail to do this, you will die" (Lev. 8:35).

On the eighth day, Moses told Aaron to offer sacrifices. He also announced the same to the Israelites. He instructed them to "present all these offerings to the LORD because the LORD will appear to you today" (Lev. 9:4). The rest of Leviticus 9 narrates how Aaron presented the offerings to God. First, he presented a sin offering for himself. He then slaughtered an animal for a burnt offering. After splashing the blood against the side of the altar, he burned each piece of the animal on the altar, but some parts he left on the altar.

After offering sacrifices for himself, he made offerings for the people. He presented a sin offering of a goat. Then he offered a burnt offering, which he mixed with a grain offering. Finally, he presented a peace offering, leaving some pieces of the animal on the altar.

Aaron then blessed the people and entered the tabernacle with Moses. When they came out, Aaron blessed the people again, at which time "the glory of the LORD appeared to the whole community" (Lev. 9:23). After that fire came from the Lord's presence and burned what was left on the altar. The people responded with worship.

Leviticus 8–9 teaches us about the beginning of the priestly work of Aaron as the high priest and of his sons. Following their ordination, they begin their work, and God reveals his glory to the people, thus confirming their status. Leviticus 10 completes this section of the book since it continues with a story about priests. It is a tough text, so rather than recounting it here, we will do so in the next chapter (70).

70. "They disobeyed the LORD by burning before him the wrong kind of fire"

» Lev. 10:1; 10:1–7

Leviticus 10 culminates the book's account of the beginning of priestly service. Leviticus 8 narrates the priests' ordination in a ritual that lasts eight days; Leviticus 9 describes them as beginning their sacrificial rituals.

Everything reported goes smoothly, but in Leviticus 10, events spiral downward. Two of Aaron's sons, Nadab and Abihu, "put coals of fire in their incense burners and sprinkled incense over them. In this way, they disobeyed the LORD by burning before him the wrong kind of fire, different than he had commanded" (10:1). As a result "fire blazed forth from the LORD's presence and burned them up, and they died there before the LORD" (10:2).

What exactly did Nadab and Abihu do to deserve God's judgment? The text simply says they offered "the wrong kind of fire" but does not specifically say what was wrong about it. The Hebrew *zarah*, translated as "wrong kind" (NLT), "unholy" (NRSVue), and "unauthorized" (NIV/ESV), often means "strange" or "foreign." The English translations here are all appropriate. The incense was the wrong kind because it was unauthorized and so was unholy. Precisely what made it "strange" is unknown because there is more than one way that the fire might be wrong or unauthorized, and therefore unholy. We are left to speculate. Perhaps the priests themselves were not authorized to offer it. Perhaps they used the wrong kind of incense (for the right kind, see Exod. 30:34–38). Perhaps they offered it at the wrong time. Perhaps they were not in the right frame of mind to offer it.

Or it could be any combination of these factors. Later in the chapter God tells Aaron that "you and your descendants must never drink wine or any other alcoholic drink before going into the Tabernacle" (Lev. 10:9). If they do, they won't be able to "distinguish between what is sacred and what is common, between what is ceremonially unclean and what is clean" (10:10). Perhaps we can infer from this that Nadab and Abihu were intoxicated as they performed their priestly duties.

At the end of Leviticus 9, God sends fire from his presence to consume the sacrifices that were offered correctly. In response to the unauthorized fire of Nadab and Abihu in the very next chapter, God sends fire that judges and kills them.

Aaron enlists two of his cousins to remove the bodies and bury them outside the camp, implying that they were unclean. Moses tells Aaron and his remaining sons not to show any visible grief at the death of Nadab and Abihu for fear of God's anger. In this way they are to demonstrate their sense that God was just in his judgment.

Moses then turns to Aaron's sons Eleazar and Ithamar to complete the sacrifices. In particular, he tells them to eat the rest of the grain offering and to do so "beside the altar" (Lev. 10:12). The breast and the thigh of the animal, however, may be eaten in any ceremonially clean location. Despite these instructions, however, Eleazar and Ithamar completely burned the sin offering and did not eat it. Moses is upset because that ritual act was to "remove the guilt of the community and to purify the people, making them right with the Lord" (Lev. 10:17). Exactly how eating the animal served this atonement function is not clear, but it may have to do with the priests taking on the guilt of the people.

Aaron responds by saying that the day's trauma kept him from eating it. He felt as if the Lord would not have been pleased if he had done so, and Moses concurs (Lev. 10:20).

LEVITICUS 11-16

Purity Laws

The next section of Leviticus concerns laws that relate to ritual purity. These include laws about food, semen, bleeding connected to a woman's reproductive system, skin disease, and mildew in houses. From a modern point of view, these are tough texts to understand. Part of the difficulty is that the text itself does not say why certain things and conditions make one unclean, so we have to make educated guesses. We assume that the priests and the people knew more than we did. In the chapters that follow, we will reflect on the possible reasons why something renders a person unclean.

It is important to understand that these things and conditions are not necessarily evil or wrong. To be ritually unclean is not the same as committing sin, though if an Israelite intentionally neglected these laws, that would be wrong. Typically, the practical effect of being unclean is that a person was not permitted to enter a holy place like the sanctuary for a period of time.

This section ends with God's instructions on how to observe the Day of Atonement (*yom kippur*). We will describe the ritual and explore the purpose of this day in chapter 74 below.

71. "By these instructions you will know what is unclean and clean, and which animals may be eaten and which may not be eaten"

» Lev. 11:47; 11:1–47

Leviticus 11 introduces laws that prohibit God's people from eating certain types of food. Most people today are familiar with the practice of orthodox Jewish people who avoid certain foods, including shellfish and pig products like ham. They do so based on traditional interpretations of the food laws (see chap. 58 for why religious Jews avoid mixing meat and dairy).

But why is consumption prohibited of these particular animals mentioned in Leviticus 11? What function did these laws serve during the Old Testament period? And why don't Christians observe these laws?

The first question of why these animals and not others requires us to make educated guesses, since nowhere is an explanation given. Many today often think these laws are guides to healthy living. But there is no reason to think this. Ham is just as healthy as lamb, for instance. Also, from a Christian point of view, if these laws intend to promote healthy eating, why are they done away with once Jesus comes?

The best explanation is that the prohibited animals seem to blur creation distinctions or are associated with death in some way. The most obvious example of blurring distinctions comes with marine animals. The acceptable animals are defined as those having fins and scales (see Lev. 11:9–12). They are fishy fish; they have the characteristics of creatures that should live in the water. But a lobster? That looks like a land animal that crawls around on the bottom of the sea.

This rationale may also operate with land animals (Lev. 11:2–8). Clean animals are those with split hooves and that chew the cud. Notice that with both marine animals and land animals, their location is a part of the description. The same is true with insects (11:20–23). Eating winged insects that walk on the ground is forbidden unless they have jointed legs to jump. In other words, winged insects that walk like land animals blur distinctions.

The rationale for clean and unclean birds seems to be different (Lev. 11:13–19). No physical characteristics are given for those birds that are acceptable; the text simply gives a list of unacceptable birds. When we read the names of the birds on the list—various types of vultures, falcons, ravens, owls, seagull, hawks, the cormorant, the stork, herons, the hoopoe, and the bat—they appear to be birds of prey, feeding on carrion. Their association with death likely renders them unclean.

In sum, the lists of unclean animals are not totally arbitrary. There are reasons for the animals that make the lists. However, these animals are not inherently bad (God created them after all) or even bad to eat (Jesus will declare them clean—see below). But the next question is, Why are there food laws anyway? How did they function during the Old Testament time period?

Israel was not the only ancient or modern culture with food laws. God often takes customs and conventions known in other cultures and uses them for his purposes. The function of food laws is to keep one group separate from other groups. If your group has food laws that prohibit certain types of food, it is really hard to sit down and have a meal with someone from another group. The purpose of food laws is thus to keep a group from fraternizing too closely with people from outside the group. Remember that God wanted his people to stay separate from other groups that worship false gods. They were to be a distinctive people who would follow God in such a winsome way that others would be attracted to join them, but they were not to go out and mingle with others for fear that they would follow in their idolatrous ways.

This leads us to our final question: Why don't Christians observe these laws today?

With the coming of Jesus, the church is called to go into the nations: "Go and make disciples of all the nations, baptizing them in the name of the Father and the Son and the Holy Spirit" (Matt. 28:19). In Christ there is no distinction between Jew and Gentile (Gal. 3:28). Jesus "united Jews and Gentiles into one people when, in his own body on the cross, he broke down the wall of hostility that separated us" (Eph. 2:14). For this reason, Christ removed the obligation not to eat food that had previously been forbidden, so Christians—whether Jewish or Gentile—can eat with each other and with others from outside the church, the lesson that Peter learned when God told him to eat with the gentile Cornelius (Acts 10–11).

72. "A man who is unclean because of an emission of semen or a woman during her menstrual period"

» Lev. 15:32–33; 12:1–8 and 15:1–33

Coming into contact with bodily fluids connected with reproduction renders a person unclean. Remember, as mentioned above, that being unclean is not the result of sin, so these laws do not imply that sex is bad or that a woman's period indicates something is wrong with her. Indeed, it may be just the opposite.

Leviticus 12 describes how a woman who has a baby is unclean for a period of time. If she has a boy, she is unclean for seven days, and then the boy is circumcised on the eighth day. Interestingly, this period of time is similar to the time period she is rendered unclean during her monthly period, and anyone who touches her during this time also becomes unclean (15:19). Leviticus 18:19 forbids having sex with a woman during this week. After birthing a boy, she is not purified from her bleeding for thirty-three days. During this time she may not go into the sanctuary or touch anything sacred.

In the case of the birth of a baby girl, everything is twice as long. The mother is unclean for two weeks rather than one and purified after sixty-six days rather than thirty-three. Whether having a boy or girl, at the end of this time the woman offers a burnt offering and a sin offering "to purify" herself (Lev. 12:7). Again, this language does not mean she has sinned; rather, there has been an interruption in her ability to enter the sacred space. We will consider why childbirth (and the menstrual cycle) renders her unclean below.

Leviticus 15:16–18 considers the man who has an emission of semen. This scenario is preceded in the broader context by a discussion of male bodily discharges and followed by the case of female bodily discharges, including her menstrual cycle. Here we focus on the emission of semen, which renders a man and the woman with whom he has had sex ritually unclean until the next evening. Clothes and leather touched by the semen will also be unclean until evening.

Again, the emission of semen under consideration here—that of marital sex—is not a sinful act. Premarital and extramarital sex are dealt with differently in the Old Testament law and include a severe set of punishments. In Deuteronomy 23:10, the law takes up the case of a nocturnal emission. The context there is purity in the battle camp (23:9), so the situation is that the man has an emission of semen in the absence of his wife. He is impure, which actually means that he could not participate in battle or stay in the camp that day since the ark of the covenant represents God.

But whatever the situation, the question remains, Why? Why do fluids (women's and men's) connected to reproduction make a person unclean? God made us sexual beings and delights in our having children, so what's the issue?

There is no question of sin here, nor are health or hygiene issues involved. We must make educated guesses. There are two possibilities, and both may be true.

On the one hand, the loss of blood and the emission of semen weaken a person, sap their vitality, and remind us of death. Holiness avoids anything connected to death, and when people come into contact with death, they cannot enter the realm of the holy. On the other hand, these fluids might be considered holy because they are associated with new life, and as such, people become unclean when they come into contact with the holy. This second explanation may also explain why the woman who has a baby girl is unclean twice as long as when she has a baby boy. The baby girl herself represents the potential of future life.

73. "It is a serious skin disease, and the priest. . . . It appears my house has some kind of mildew"

» Lev. 13:3 and 14:35; 13:1–14:57

Lepers in the New Testament often approached Jesus asking to be cleansed of their condition. On one occasion, Jesus told the healed person to go to the priest and give the offering "required in the law of Moses" (Mark 1:44). Jesus here refers to Leviticus 14:2–32. For this reason, some people think the skin disease at issue in Leviticus 13–14 is specifically and exclusively leprosy. They also think that these laws concern public health because they declare the diseased person ritually unclean and require separation from the community.

This is wrong for a number of reasons. First, leprosy (Hansen's disease) is not that contagious. Until recently it was thought to be, but now we know it is not. Leprosy disfigures a person but not directly due to the disease. People with leprosy lose their sense of touch, so they don't react to pain, compromising their bodies when they don't sense injury. However, it is very possible that ancient people thought the disease was contagious, and God could have condescended to their understanding through this law. Second and more determinative, the Hebrew word used in Leviticus does not mean leprosy but rather any skin disease, whether contagious or not.

People with a skin disease reported their condition to a priest, who would examine the person's body and then determine whether they were clean or unclean. Not all manifestations of skin disease rendered a person unclean, but only "if the hair in the affected area has turned white and the problem appears to be more than skin-deep" (Lev. 13:3). If these conditions don't pertain, then the person with the skin disease will be quarantined for a week and inspected again. If there is no further problem, a second week of quarantine follows. If the skin disease is improving, they may return to the community.

Leviticus 13 presents several scenarios that require screening and pronouncement by the priest. If the person is unclean, then they must tear their clothing, not comb their hair, cover their mouth, and call out "Unclean! Unclean!" And "they must live in isolation in their place outside the camp" (13:45–46).

But if hygiene is not the reason for these laws, what is? An often-overlooked paragraph in Leviticus 13 might help answer this question. Leviticus 13:12–17 asks about the case where a person is covered "from head to foot" with skin disease. The priest declares this person "clean." The exception is if the person has open sores.

This surprising case helps us see the symbolic meaning behind these laws. A person is clean if they have no skin disease or if they are completely covered by skin disease. They are whole. If they are partially covered by skin disease they lack wholeness. Though the word is not used in the chapter, the Hebrew word for whole is *shalom*, which most people know as the Hebrew word for peace.

There might be a second symbolic meaning. Contact with death in certain situations renders a person unclean. Somebody who has a skin disease that partially covers their body is analogous to a person whose body experiences decay, which is associated with death (though this does not explain why a person whose whole body is covered is considered "clean").

Clothes (Lev. 13:47–59) and houses (14:33–53) can have a condition similar to skin disease. Indeed, the Hebrew word translated earlier as "skin disease" (*tsara'at*) is applied in this context to clothes and houses (14:34, 44, 55), though of course "skin disease" is not a possible translation (though the ESV does, unfortunately, translate *tsara'at* as "leprous disease"). Translations rightly render the word either "mildew" (NLT) or "mold" (NIV). Mildew and mold are both fungi that spread through microscopic spores that then bloom in wet places. Clothes and structures can develop mildew or mold. Clothes and houses that have mildew or mold are "unclean." The result is the burning of the clothes and the removal of molded/mildewed stones from the house. If the house is seriously compromised, then it must be torn down and the stones taken out of the town.

74. "The scapegoat chosen by lot"

» Lev. 16:10; 16:1–34

The final chapter of this section concerning purity appropriately describes a vital ritual called the Day of Atonement (*yom kippur*). Most people know about this day because it has played an extremely important role in Jewish life up to the present time. While the purpose of the ritual remains largely the same as it was during the biblical period, the manner in which it is observed has changed. With the destruction of the Second Temple by the Romans in AD 70, sacrifices can no longer be offered. This chapter concerns the description of its observance in Leviticus 16, not its modern-day equivalent.

Leviticus 16 gives a detailed description of the rituals for the day. Some questions about these rituals cannot be resolved with great certainty, including those surrounding the so-called scapegoat.

The Day of Atonement is the only day when a person—specifically, the high priest—may enter the Most Holy Place of the sanctuary, and great care must be taken. The high priest begins by removing his ornate priestly garments and instead wearing linen clothes, likely reflecting humility. Before he puts on this clothing, he washes himself, perhaps symbolic of moving into the realm of the sacred or holy. He first brings a ram and a young bull for a burnt offering for himself, and for the Israelite community he brings two male goats for a sin offering and a ram for a burnt offering.

The sacrifice of the bull makes atonement for the priest and his family. Then the priest takes the two goats, which he presents "to the LORD at the entrance of the Tabernacle" (Lev. 16:7). He casts lots concerning the two goats. The lots will designate one goat "for the LORD" and the other "for the scapegoat" (16:8), according to the NIV translation. This translation is not misleading; the goat will function as a scapegoat, taking the sins of the Israelites and bearing them away from the tabernacle and into the wilderness. But the NIV obscures an issue; the ESV and NRSVue say the goat is "for Azazel." *'Aza'zel* is the Hebrew word for scapegoat, and there is a question about what that Hebrew word means.

But first, let's continue to follow the ritual. Aaron sacrifices the goat chosen "for the LORD" for the purpose of making atonement, but then he sends the second goat into the wilderness. Before Aaron sends out this second goat, the scapegoat, he is to finish making atonement for the tabernacle and then lay his hands on the goat "and confess over it all the wickedness, rebellion, and sins of the people of Israel" (Lev. 16:21). In this way the goat takes the sins that have accumulated in the tabernacle for the year and carries them away. The idea is that throughout the year individual Israelites have been coming with their sin to make atonement. They have ritually transferred their sin to the animals that are then sacrificed, their blood sprinkled on the tabernacle itself. In this way, symbolically the tabernacle itself has accumulated the sins of the people. Now, through the scapegoat, the sins of Israel are carried off into the wilderness.

But back to the word *'aza'zel*, which only appears in Leviticus 16:8, 10, 26. The function of the second goat is well communicated by the translation "scapegoat," and some think that the word is a compound of two Hebrew words meaning "goat" and "go away." Others think *'aza'zel* is the name of a place in the wilderness. The most likely explanation is that *'aza'zel* is the name of a supernatural being, probably a demon. This understanding is supported by the parallel between the first goat "for the LORD" and the second one "for Azazel." If this is the case, we shouldn't think of the goat as an offering to a demon; indeed, offerings to goat demons are forbidden in the very next chapter (17:7). Rather, the idea is that sin is being sent to the realm where it belongs.

After sending out the scapegoat, Aaron takes off the linen priestly garments, bathes himself, and then dresses again in his ornate outfit. He then offers more sacrifices for himself and the community. In this way, the high priest has completed the ritual that has removed the sins that have accumulated at the tabernacle over the past year.

LEVITICUS 17-27

The Holiness Code

The last part of Leviticus contains laws of various sorts. It is often called the Holiness Code because holiness is an emphasis. The word "holy" occurs numerous times, most notably the exhortations to "be holy, because I, the LORD your God, am holy" (Lev. 19:2; cf. 20:26) and "set yourselves apart to be holy, for I am the LORD your God" (20:7). The frequent message is that God is the one who ultimately makes a person holy (20:8; 21:15, 23; 22:9, 16).

Leviticus 17 presents laws that have to do with the proper handling of blood and the slaughter of animals. All sacrifices must happen at the tabernacle and nowhere else (Lev. 17:3–9). Eating blood is forbidden (17:10–12), including that of hunted animals (17:13–14). People who eat any wild animals found dead will be unclean until evening (17:15–16).

Leviticus 18–20 contains laws to live as holy people. These laws are of various sorts, but sexual laws and laws against false worship abound. In the former category are prohibitions against adultery, different forms of incest, bestiality, and same-sex relations, as well as having intercourse with a woman who is having her period. The laws against false worship include regulations for proper sacrifice and prohibition of making idols. Some laws, such as honoring parents and not stealing or lying, are similar to the Ten Commandments. Other laws prohibit certain types of mixtures (see chap. 75).

Leviticus 21–22 has laws specifically directed to priests. These include commands not to touch a corpse, except for that of a close relative. Priests must not shave their hair, edge their beard, or intentionally cut themselves. They must only marry virgins.

Leviticus 23 and following address the whole community of Israel, beginning by describing the Sabbath and the annual festivals. Leviticus 24:1–9 instructs Moses to have the Israelites bring olive oil and bread for use in the tabernacle. The end of the chapter (24:10–23) narrates the account of a blasphemer's execution.

Leviticus 25 explains how the Sabbatical Year and the Year of Jubilee should be celebrated. Leviticus 26:1–13 lists blessings for those who obey the law, while 26:14–46 details curses or punishments that result from disobedience. Rewards and punishments follow the giving of the law in the book of Deuteronomy as well and align with the pattern of ancient Near Eastern treaties, which provide the cultural background to biblical covenants (see the introduction to the book of Deuteronomy).

Leviticus ends with a chapter on various types of voluntary and nonvoluntary offerings (Lev. 27:1–33). The final verse summarizes the book: "These are the commands that the Lord gave through Moses on Mount Sinai for the Israelites" (27:34).

75. "Do not mate two different kinds of animals. Do not plant your field with two different kinds of seed. Do not wear clothing woven from two different kinds of thread."

» Lev. 19:19

Leviticus 19:19 forbids three types of mixture: breeding two different animals, planting a field with two types of seed, or wearing clothing made with two types of material. Deuteronomy 22:9–11 similarly prohibits planting two types of seeds in a vineyard, plowing with an ox and donkey yoked together, and wearing clothes made of wool and linen.

Why are these mixtures prohibited, and why do Christians today ignore all these laws? The answers to these two questions are related.

The text doesn't explicitly state the reason for these commands, but thinking about them in the context of the Torah's teaching about what makes something unclean or impure provides a reasonable answer. In chapter 71, we looked at laws concerning clean and unclean animals and suggested that one of the principles separating clean from unclean is that the clean animals fit properly in their creation category. Clean fish had fins and scales; they were fishy fish. Lobsters and shrimp did not fit as well with their watery environment. Confusing creation categories signaled something as unclean.

Mixing animals, seeds, and different types of materials blurred categories as well. Hybrids were unclean in the symbolic ritual world of the Old Testament. In this way, God taught his people that they needed to stay separate and not mix with idolatrous people. This distinction is often described as Israelites needing to stay separate from gentiles, but ultimately this is not an ethnic distinction since gentiles could join God's people by rejecting their false gods and embracing Yahweh (e.g., Rahab, Ruth, and others).

As with the food laws, there is nothing inherently wrong with mixing animals, seeds, or different types of material. God constructs this symbolic ritual world in order to teach his people to stay holy—that is, separate from those who might persuade them to worship idols.

Thus, as with the food laws, once Jesus comes and tears down "the wall of hostility that separated" Jews and gentiles (Eph. 2:14), the laws concerning mixtures are no longer relevant and so are not observed by Christians.

Sometimes mixtures seem to mark something as holy rather than unclean. The cherubim, those powerful spiritual beings who stand closest to the presence of God, are often described as a hybrid of different animals. Ezekiel, for instance, describes them as having a human form, but with four faces, four wings, and feet like a calf. The four faces were those of a human bèing, a lion, an ox, and an eagle (Ezek. 1:4–14). Priests' clothes and the innermost curtain of the tabernacle were also woven with different types of material (Exod. 26:1, 31; 28:6, 15; 39:29). Thus, another reason why mixtures may have been forbidden was because certain types were reserved for the realm of the holy.

76. "An eye for an eye"

» Lev. 24:20

See chapter 56.

77. "Then you will eat the flesh of your own sons and daughters"

» Lev. 26:29

See chapter 107.

The Book of Numbers

The book of Numbers picks up the narrative where Leviticus leaves off. Remember that the Torah—also called the Pentateuch ("five scrolls")—is a single literary composition in its final form, not five separate books. Though a single composition, no one scroll could hold such a lengthy text, so it was divided into five parts. Numbers is the fourth part, and its first section (Num. 1:1–10:10) takes place over a nineteen-day period, beginning more than a year after Israel had departed Egypt (1:1; 10:11). During this time, the Israelites prepare for the march in the wilderness.

The book of Numbers pictures the Israelites in the wilderness as an army. Accordingly, the first chapter recounts a military census (men over twenty able to serve) of those who have come out of Egypt. The layout of their camp is strikingly similar to that of an ancient Near Eastern war camp (Num. 2). The tabernacle is in the center where the war leader's tent would be located. The Levites camp around the tabernacle, occupying the space of the king's personal retinue or bodyguards. Then the other tribes have their assigned places to the east, south, west, and north of the tabernacle, just as an army would be situated all around the king's tent.

Numbers 3–4 describes the duties of the Levitical clans responsible for transport of the tabernacle (see chap. 78). Numbers

5–6 includes laws connected to a woman suspected of adultery (see chap. 79) and to the Nazirite (see chap. 80), as well as instructions for the high priest to bless the Israelites.

During this period of preparation for wilderness travel, the various tribes offer gifts at the dedication of the tabernacle (Num. 7). The Lord gives Moses additional instructions for maintaining the tabernacle (Num. 8–9), and the people celebrate the Passover (9:1–14). In Numbers 9:15–23, the cloud representing God's presence settles over the tabernacle. The final section of this first part of Numbers is instructions for making and using two trumpets to signal assembling and marching commands during Israel's journey through the wilderness.

After these preparations the Israelites set out from the Desert of Sinai, initiating the second section of Numbers (10:11–25:18). These chapters narrate events that take place during the wilderness journey. Most describe rebellions against the leadership or against God himself. The people complain about the lack and quality of food and water (11:1–35). Miriam and Aaron complain about Moses's leadership (12:1–16). The spies bring back a report about the land that frightens the people, who respond with a lack of trust in God (13:1–14:45). Korah and others rebel against Moses's leadership (16:1–50). Tribal leaders protest Aaron's special position as high priest (17:1–13; see chap. 82). Moses and Aaron anger God by striking a rock to bring water (20:1–13; see chap. 83). Some Israelites get seduced into worshiping foreign gods (25:1–18). Indeed, these episodes (especially Num. 13–14) explain why Israel spent forty years in the wilderness.

Numbers 10:11–25:18 also includes some additional laws (15:1–41; 18:1–19:22), as well as an account of the Israelites' passage through the Transjordan regions of Edom and Moab. In the context of the latter, a prophet named Balaam is hired by the Moabite king Barak to curse the Israelites (22:1–24:25; see chap. 85). Still, these chapters' main message is the infidelity of the "first generation," the adults who came out of Egypt. Because they lacked faith, God declares they will die in the wilderness, thus dooming them to a forty-year sojourn.

Numbers 26 is a turning point. This chapter recounts a second military census (26:2). This census counts the second generation, those who were not adults at the exodus and those born in the wilderness. This census signals that the forty years of wandering are nearing an end. The first generation doomed to die in the wilderness has passed away, and the second prepares to enter the land. From this point, the book moves on from the turmoil and rebellion of the earlier chapters. In Deuteronomy, the book that follows Numbers, Moses exhorts this second generation as it prepares to enter the land, telling them to be faithful in a way their parents were not.

The concluding chapters of Numbers include laws about inheritance (Num. 27:1–11; 36:1–13), presenting various offerings to God (28:1–40), and vows (30:13). The chapters also look ahead, as Joshua is chosen to succeed Moses as Israel's leader (27:12–23). The people defeat the Midianites (31:1–54), and the land in the Transjordan is given to the tribes of Reuben, Gad, and half the tribe of Manasseh, though they promise to join their fellow tribes in the conquest of Canaan (32:1–42). There is also a summarizing itinerary of the wilderness journey (34:1–15) and an anticipation of the division of the land among the tribes (34:16–29). The narrator reports that the Lord designated certain towns for the Levites (35:1–8) and as cities of refuge (35:9–34).

78. "The duties of the Kohathites . . . Gershonites. . . . the Merarite division"

» Num. 4:4, 24, 29; 4:1–49

The tabernacle was a tent for the divine king (see "Exodus 25–40: Building the Tabernacle" and chaps. 59–62). God had Israel build it while they were in the wilderness. The Israelites themselves were living in tents, which they needed to pack up and move as they went from place to place. That would be true for God's tent as well. Even after Israel entered the promised land, the tabernacle still moved from place to place, though it was located at various places for long periods of time (e.g., Gibeon, Shiloh). This situation would not change until Solomon built the temple (see chap. 91).

Numbers 4 assigns three clans of Levites to do the work of taking down the tabernacle and putting it up again. The first was the Kohathite clan, responsible for carrying the sacred objects inside the tabernacle from place to place (4:1–20). However, they were not the ones to pack up these objects. Aaron's son Eleazar was in charge of that aspect of the work. Aaron and his sons would go into the tabernacle and carefully use the inner curtain that overhung the tabernacle walls to pack up the ark of the covenant, the most holy object in the tabernacle, and then insert its carrying poles. Other precious fabric of different colors was used to cover the table of the bread of presence, the lampstand (menorah), the gold incense altar, the various utensils like bowls, ladles, jars and pitchers, and so forth. They would then cover these precious fabrics with the more durable "fine goatskin leather" (Num. 4:6, 8, 12–14). The priests also prepared the outside bronze altar and its accoutrements for travel.

Aaron and his sons had to do the packing because other Levites, including the Kohathites, were never permitted inside the Holy Place. Indeed, the "Kohathites will come and carry these things to the next destination. But they must not touch the sacred objects, or they will die" (Num. 4:15).

The Gershonites were "responsible for general service and carrying loads" (Num. 4:24). Their tasks include carrying the curtains of the tabernacle and the courtyard, the tabernacle itself, the ropes, and everything associated with their use (4:24–26). Ithamar, another son of Aaron, was in charge of them, but the Gershonites could do their own packing because, though the tabernacle equipment was sacred, it was not as sacred as the items in the tabernacle.

The third clan was the Merarites, also under the leadership of Ithamar (Num. 4:29–33). These priests were responsible to carry the framework for the tabernacle and its courtyard: crossbars, posts, bases, pegs, ropes, and all the related accessories.

All this work was necessary and important, but there is one question to ask. Even though Aaron and his sons packed the furniture and articles inside the tabernacle, Hebrews 9:7 indicates that "only the high priest ever entered the Most Holy Place, and only once a year." This refers to the Day of Atonement described in Leviticus 16 (see chap. 74). God instructed Moses to "warn your brother, Aaron, not to enter the Most Holy Place behind the inner curtain whenever he chooses; if he does, he will die" (16:2). A Jewish legend, first encountered in the thirteenth-century Zohar (literature on the Jewish mysticism of Kabbalah), says that the high priest would enter on this occasion with a rope around his ankle because if he were to die inside the tabernacle, they would have to drag his body out! This practice likely did not take place during biblical times, but it drives the point home.

How then could Aaron and his sons enter the Most Holy Place in order to pack up the ark that was there? We can only speculate, but we do so based on ancient Near Eastern parallels. Sumerian, Babylonian, and Assyrian temples were also considered holy places since the statues of their gods were inside representing the gods' presence. When a temple had to be torn down and rebuilt, in order not to offend the gods the priests would perform a ritual that in essence decommissioned the temple until a new temple was built on the same location. Once the new temple was built, a ritual was performed to announce the return of holiness to the location. Perhaps before the Levites packed up the tabernacle and Aaron or his sons went in to begin the process, a ritual was performed to deconsecrate the site, and then when the tabernacle was set up again, the priests performed another ritual to signal that the site was holy.

79. "Suppose a man's wife goes astray"

» Num. 5:12; 5:11–31

Numbers 5 describes a ritual enacted when a man suspects his wife has committed adultery (5:11–31). The logic of the ritual is easy to follow, but it is also contrary to modern sensibilities and involves supernatural intervention in such a way that it becomes a difficult text for many modern readers. We start by simply describing the situation and the ritual itself as the biblical text describes them.

The situation is that a man suspects his wife has committed adultery, and he grows jealous. There are no witnesses or evidence, so he cannot accuse her formally, but he still suspects her of infidelity.

In this case, he takes her to the priest along with "a jealousy offering—an offering to prove whether or not she is guilty" (Num. 5:15). He gives the priest the offering, which is two quarts of barley flour with no olive oil or incense added. This offering in part is payment for the priest who conducts the ritual, though a portion of the offering is burned for a memorial offering (5:26).

The priest then loosens the woman's hair and mixes holy water with dust from the tabernacle floor. He informs her that if she is not guilty of adultery, nothing will happen to her. However, if she is guilty, then, to translate Numbers 5:22 a bit woodenly, "her belly will swell and her thigh will fall away." Virtually all interpreters and many translations (like the NLT) make it clear that the thigh is a euphemism for the womb, and the meaning is that the woman, if she is pregnant, will miscarry (as the NIV and other translations make clear). The priest writes this curse on a scroll and then washes the words off the scroll with water into the cup. He then makes the woman drink the concoction.

Many modern readers find this ritual problematic if not repulsive for more than one reason. First, the ritual seems to oppress women. Why isn't there a similar ritual for a man suspected of adultery? Second, if the woman is guilty, then the life of the baby in the womb is put to an end. On the one hand, the text upsets today's advocates of women's rights. On the other hand, the ritual can offend those who are prolife.

There is no easy response to either of these reactions, but we should try to understand the text in its original setting. The first thing to note is that God is in control. The logic of the text depends on the fact that only the guilty will suffer the negative consequences. Even if she is not pregnant at the time, the ritual results in her not being able to have children in the future (Num. 6:22). The second consideration is that the ritual is performed when the husband is jealous and suspects adultery. If the woman is innocent, the man might remain jealous if God didn't settle the matter, and this ritual resolves the issue. In this way, the ritual is in the woman's interest. A third consideration is that the ultimate concern of the ritual is paternity since children inherit from their fathers. If the child is another man's, that creates a problem. This third consideration is almost certainly why there is not a comparable ritual for a man suspected of adultery. We should also remember that adultery of a man or a woman is punishable by death (Lev. 20:10), so a man who commits adultery does not escape serious consequences (even if he is allowed to live). And from this text, it does not appear that the woman exposed by this ritual was put to death.

For a final thought about this difficult passage, consider the context of the broader ancient Near East, especially Mesopotamia, which exhibits similarities with certain ordeal rituals. The most interesting are those that concern a suspected witch or sorcerer. If a person were suspected of witchcraft, he or she would be taken to a river and thrown into it. If the person was carried away by the waters and drowned, they were a witch or sorcerer. If the person was innocent, they would survive.

While there are similarities between the biblical ritual and the Mesopotamian water ordeal, there was also a crucial difference. In the latter, the gods who oversaw the ritual were false gods. The outcomes then would be arbitrary. Yahweh oversaw the biblical ordeal and so the results reflected the truth of the matter.

80. "The special vow of a Nazirite"

» Num. 6:2; 6:1–21

Numbers 6 gives instructions for taking a vow to become a Nazirite. The passage never explains the role or status of a Nazirite, most likely because the original audience already knew. Nonetheless, we can have a pretty good idea of the Nazirite's status, and after looking at the steps a person must take to become a Nazirite, we will make our suggestion.

To take the vow of the Nazirite, a man or a woman must not drink alcohol. They can't drink vinegar made from wine or even grape juice. Furthermore, they can't eat grapes, raisins, or anything associated with a grapevine (Num. 6:3–4).

Nazirites can't go anywhere near a dead body, even if the dead person is a close relative like a father or a son or a sister (Num. 6:6–8). Doing so would compromise their vow. This is true even if someone suddenly and without warning drops dead next to them (6:7).

The most distinctive part of the Nazirite vow is that they must not cut their hair (Num. 6:5). Their long hair is a visible sign of their vow. If they compromise their vow by coming into contact with a corpse, they have to wait seven days and then shave their head. At that time, the Nazirite makes an offering to recommit themselves to their vow.

This recommitment took place at the tabernacle, presumably in the presence of the priests (Num. 6:10, 11), so the original vow was likely taken at the sanctuary as well. Indeed, the instructions for the Nazirites reveal a connection here with priests. By taking the vow, the Nazirite, who is not a priest or a Levite, promises to abide by the rules that priests follow but even more intensely.

A priest may not touch a dead body without becoming unclean unless the corpse is that of an immediate relative (Lev. 21:1–4). An ordinary Israelite may drink alcohol, but priests must not drink alcohol when performing their duties (Ezek. 44:21), though even priests may drink alcohol when off duty. A Nazirite may not drink alcohol at any time or even eat or drink anything connected to the grapevine.

The instruction concerning the hair may also be connected to priestly instruction, though this is less clear. Priests were not to shave their heads or shave off the edges of their beards (Lev. 21:5), but a person could not cut their hair at any time while under a Nazirite vow. Cut hair is dead matter, so to cut one's hair brings one into contact with something dead.

Thus, a Nazirite is a person who for reasons of special dedication to God takes a temporary vow to live for a period of time like a priest, only more so. However, there is no indication that they functioned like a priest or served at the tabernacle.

The Old Testament writers tell us about two men who are Nazirites, Samuel and Samson. We will return to their stories in a later volume, but their status raises some questions. For one thing, they did not take the vow; their mothers dedicated them at birth. Second, unlike the temporary vow in Numbers, Samuel and Samson were Nazirites for life. Apparently there were variations on the Nazirite vow not explicitly described in Numbers.

81. "We saw the Nephilim there"

» Num. 13:33 (NIV); 13:31–33

In Numbers 13, the Israelites are nearing the promised land as they camp at Kadesh-barnea in the Desert of Paran. From there,

Moses sends twelve spies into the land of Canaan, one spy from each tribe, to report back on what they see. What is the land like? What are the people like? Are they weak or are they strong? The spies were also to try to bring back some of the produce of the land.

The spies do as instructed, returning to Moses with a positive-negative report. The land is amazing, "flowing with milk and honey" (Num. 13:27)—that is, a luxurious and productive land. But fearsome and formidable enemies live there. In particular, the dangerous Amalekites (see chap. 105) live in the land. Caleb, the representative of Judah and one of only two faithful spies (the other being Joshua), insists that Israel can nonetheless possess the land (13:30). For their faithful response in contrast to the other spies, he and Joshua will be the only two adults who left Egypt permitted to enter the land.

In spite of Caleb's confidence, the other spies object and say, "We can't go up against them! They are stronger than we are!" (Num. 13:31). Then they up the ante. They report that they saw the Nephilim there. They are "giants," and "we felt like grasshoppers, and that's what they thought, too!" (13:33).

The mention of Nephilim brings to mind Genesis 6:1–4 (see chap. 13), the only other place where we find this term. But the story in Genesis 6 happens before the flood. Are we to think that the Nephilim survived the flood? Some readers believe that the mention of Nephilim here in Numbers means that they did manage to survive the flood. Some even believe that their ability to survive the flood indicates that they are angels, though fallen angels to be sure (the word Nephilim means "fallen ones"). But even though some early Jewish legends take that approach, these arguments are unlikely, and there is a better explanation for the presence of a group called the Nephilim in the land at the time of the exodus.

Rather than thinking the Nephilim survived the flood or that these were fallen angels, it is more likely that the Israelite spies were so overwhelmed by the size of these people that they associated them with the "heroes and famous warriors of ancient times," the Nephilim of Genesis 6:4.

82. "Aaron's staff . . . had sprouted, budded, blossomed, and produced ripe almonds!"

» Num. 17:8; 17:1–13

The book of Numbers chronicles Israel's shaky relationship with God in the wilderness. Besides conflicts between God and the people (Num. 11; 13–14), several stories recount conflicts between people, particularly among leaders. In Numbers 12, Miriam and Aaron question and challenge Moses's leadership. In Numbers 16, Korah and others oppose Moses and Aaron. In the present episode, the tribal leaders of the other eleven tribes question the status of Aaron and the tribe of the Levites.

God instructs Moses to have the twelve tribal leaders bring their walking staffs to him. Moses then places the staffs "in the LORD's presence in the Tabernacle of the Covenant" (Num. 17:7). The next day, they returned and found that of the twelve staffs, only Aaron's "had sprouted, budded, blossomed, and produced ripe almonds!" (17:8), obviously indicating that indeed the Lord had chosen Aaron and his tribe for special service before the Lord. Accordingly, God told Moses to place the budding staff in front of the ark as a warning to those who grumbled about God's choice of Aaron and the Levites.

All of this is relatively straightforward, but why does God demonstrate his choice of the Levitical tribe in this particular way? Answering this question helps us see the significance of the staff as a symbol of God's presence.

We start with the lampstand or menorah that was placed in the tabernacle (Exod. 25:31–39; see chap. 60). Interestingly, the description makes it sound like a flowering tree with branches, buds, and blossoms. Specifically, the menorah is likened to an almond tree: "Craft the center stem of the lampstand with four lamp cups shaped like almond blossoms, complete with buds and petals" (25:34).

The presence of a tree in the tabernacle where God makes his presence known among his people clearly echoes the tree of life in the garden of Eden. The tabernacle is a little bit of Eden on earth, where God makes his presence known freely among his people.

Thus, Aaron's rod, budding with almond blossoms, is intended to show that God was present with Aaron and his tribe in a special way. It also meant the Levites could serve God in his very presence.

83. "Then Moses raised his hand and struck the rock twice with the staff"

» Num. 20:11; 20:1–13

There are two instances when Moses strikes a rock and God provides water for the people in the wilderness. The first time is in Exodus 17 and it puts the Israelites in a bad light. When they camp at a place called Rephidim, they complain to Moses about a lack of water. Earlier, in Exodus 16, they had complained about a lack of food, and now they grumble about water. Moses criticizes them for complaining and accuses them of testing the Lord (17:2). From Moses's reaction it seems as if he expected them to simply wait and trust God to supply the water they needed, but they don't, and Moses complains to God about them.

God instructs Moses to take the staff with which he struck the waters of the Nile, turning it into blood, and to strike the rock at Mount Sinai (Exod. 17:5). He obeys God's instructions and water gushes out. Moses then names the place Massah ("test") and Meribah ("arguing"), because the Israelites argued and tested the Lord at that place.

The second time Moses strikes a rock (Num. 20), the action puts both Moses and the people in a bad light. Indeed, Moses's actions this time disqualify him from entering the promised land. The first impression may be that Moses's words and actions don't seem that bad. One wonders why God gets so upset. But a closer look reveals the problem.

Israel arrives at Kadesh, and again there is no water. The people rebel against Moses and Aaron for bringing them to a place with nothing to drink. As before, Moses and Aaron take the problem to God, who instructs them to take the staff but this time to speak to the rock. If they do, then the rock will provide "enough water . . . to satisfy the whole community and their livestock" (Num. 20:8).

When Moses gets his rod and appears before the people, he is obviously still angry with them. He shouts at them: "Listen, you rebels! Must we bring you water from this rock?" (Num. 20:10). Then, rather than speaking to the rock, he strikes it twice. God is not happy with Moses and Aaron and says, "Because you did not trust me enough to demonstrate my holiness to the people of Israel, you will not lead them into the land I am giving them!" (20:12).

But what exactly did Moses and Aaron do that was so wrong? First, they did not obey God's clear instructions, striking the rock rather than speaking to it. It is also possible that the rock represents God (see 1 Cor. 10:4), so Moses may be venting his anger against God himself. Perhaps even more egregious, rather than giving glory to God, Moses and Aaron attribute the provision of water to themselves rather than to him when they say, "Must *we* bring you water from this rock?"

Thus, Moses and Aaron may not enter the promised land. Aaron dies first (Num. 20:22–29). Moses is allowed to go with the Israelites all the way to the border of the promised land, where God allows him to ascend Pisgah Peak on Mount Nebo and look into the land before he dies (Deut. 34:1–8). While not perfect, Moses was nonetheless a great leader whom God honored (34:10–12).

84. "Make a replica of a poisonous snake and attach it to a pole"

» Num. 21:8; 21:4–9

The Israelites who left Egypt as adults continued to complain and grumble. As they set out from Mount Hor, they are sick and tired of the journey, forgetting that it was their rebellion against God that led to the long journey and God's judgment that their generation would die in the wilderness.

In this episode, they are complaining about Moses and God, again protesting the lack of food and water. They have food—God provides daily manna after all—but they hate it. God responds by sending poisonous snakes that bite the people, leading them to repent.

Moses again intercedes for them. God hears his prayer and tells Moses to make a replica of a poisonous snake and put it on a pole. When bitten by the snakes, the Israelites could look at the bronze snake and be healed.

The storyline of this episode is easy to follow. What makes the bronze snake a tough text is that it looks like a form of sympathetic magic. In sympathetic magic, one makes an object that resembles in some way the harm that one wants to ward off or remedy. In this case, healing from a snake bite is accomplished by looking at a bronze snake. However, though the bronze snake looks like an object of sympathetic magic, it only works because God wills it.

But why bother with a bronze serpent? God could simply heal people without having them look at a snake. However, the Israelites can learn a lesson by the presence of this bronze serpent. Every time they see it (and it was present beyond this event), it should remind them of the consequences of rebelling against God. It is a tangible reminder that they need to trust God.

This was the likely intention for the use of the bronze snake, but the people end up misusing it. Centuries later, King Hezekiah (reigned ca. 715–686 BC) restored proper worship practices in Judah. As part of this, he "broke up the bronze serpent that Moses had made, because the people of Israel had been offering sacrifices to it. The bronze serpent was called Nehushtan" (2 Kings 18:4). *Nehushtan* sounds like the Hebrew words for both "bronze" and "snake." That the Israelites treated it as an idol shows that sinful people can misuse even good things for evil purposes.

85. "Then the LORD gave the donkey the ability to speak"

» Num. 22:28; 22:21–41

Balaam is one of the most interesting characters in the Torah. He is a foreign prophet hired by Balak, king of Moab, to curse the Israelites who were traveling from the wilderness through his kingdom. He wasn't so much worried about them fighting as he was about their depletion of his country's food resources (Num. 22:4).

Balaam was a well-known prophet in the region. Archaeologists have discovered an inscription that mentions Balaam son of Beor, "a divine seer" (*COS* 2.27:142), at a site called Deir 'Alla, about thirty miles from present-day Amman, Jordan. Though this text dates between 800 and 650 BC and so is well after the events in Numbers, it demonstrates that Balaam left his imprint on the local cultural memory.

Balak hired Balaam to curse Israel through ritual means, but before Balaam could do so, God spoke to him. Most memorable is the scene where Balaam receives his assignment from Balak and starts on his journey toward Moab to meet the king. Previously, God had told the prophet not to go to Moab, and so he had refused the offer. But when Balak's messengers returned and sweetened the deal, God told Balaam he could go, but "do only what I tell you to do" (Num. 22:20).

Even so, as Balaam sets out on his donkey with the Moabite officials, God is angry with him (Num. 22:22). Perhaps God suspects that Balaam will not follow his instructions, and he wants to give him a lesson to make sure that he does. The angel of the Lord, unseen by Balaam, stands with a drawn sword in front of the donkey. The donkey takes off across the open field to Balaam's great frustration. That the donkey saw the angel while Balaam did not illustrates Balaam's lack of spiritual perception.

After beating the animal, Balaam sets out again, but this time the angel places himself in a narrow spot between two walls, with the result that the donkey crushes Balaam's foot against a wall as it squeezes by. Again, Balaam beats the animal. The third time the angel positions himself in an even narrower spot so that the donkey simply lies down. This time when Balaam beats the donkey God gives it the ability to talk, and the donkey complains about the beatings. At that point, God opens Balaam's eyes so he too sees the angel, who tells the diviner/prophet that if the donkey had not stopped, the angel would have killed Balaam.

The messenger again warns Balaam to do only what God tells him to do. Thus, when Balaam arrives in Moab and Balak tells him to curse Israel, God only lets him bless them. Indeed, Balaam blesses the Israelites four times at God's command. The fourth is the most dramatic:

> I see him, but not here and now.
>   I perceive him, but far in the distant future.
> A star will rise from Jacob;
>   a scepter will emerge from Israel. (Num. 24:17)

Since the scepter was the symbol of royalty, this blessing anticipates the emergence of kingship in Israel.

God frustrated Balak's intention to curse Israel, as well as Balaam's hope of receiving a large sum of money for his work. However, Balaam found a way to get paid when he devised a strategy to send pagan women among the Israelites to tempt them away from their worship of the Lord (Num. 25; for Balaam's involvement see Num. 31:16; Jude 1:11; Rev. 2:14).

Many readers today find Balaam's talking donkey hard to believe since it sounds more like a fable than history. However, God can use whatever mouthpiece he so chooses.

The Book of Deuteronomy

The fifth and final book of the Torah is Deuteronomy. The Torah, also called the Pentateuch ("five scrolls"), is a single literary whole divided into five parts because a single scroll could not hold the entire document.

Although part of the larger Torah, Deuteronomy also has its own literary integrity. The book contains the final speech Moses delivered to the Israelites on the plain of Moab, east of the Jordan River, just before they entered the promised land. These Israelites were the second generation out of Egypt, since their fathers and mothers, the ones who left Egypt as adults, died in the wilderness as judgment for not trusting God. Only Joshua and Caleb are allowed to enter the land (see chap. 81). Not even Moses will enter the land due to his sin of striking the rock to get water in Numbers 20:1–13 (see chap. 83). The purpose of Moses's sermon in Deuteronomy is to warn the second generation to remain faithful to God and not sin as their parents had. This purpose is served in part by Moses reminding the people of the law, starting with the Ten Commandments. Thus, the book is named Deuteronomy or "second (giving of the) law."

The structure of Deuteronomy resembles an ancient Near Eastern treaty, in particular a vassal treaty. In such a treaty, the king of a powerful nation (a suzerain) enters into an agreement with a lesser nation (a vassal). This type of treaty has five parts, which Deuteronomy mirrors. Deuteronomy is not a treaty, but it is a report of Moses leading Israel in a renewal of a covenant, and all five parts of a vassal treaty are evident in Deuteronomy.

1. *Preamble*. The treaty begins by introducing the great king and his vassal counterpart. In the case of Deuteronomy, God is the great king and Israel is his vassal people. Moses functions as a mediator of the treaty (Deut. 1:1–8).
2. *Historical prologue*. This section rehearses the relationship between the great king and his vassal nation from the past up to the present moment. The emphasis is on how good the great king has been to his vassal. In Deuteronomy, the historical prologue continues from Deuteronomy 1:9 through the end of Deuteronomy 3.
3. *Laws or stipulations of the treaty*. The third section contains laws the vassal must obey to maintain a relationship with the great king. The historical prologue has laid the groundwork for the law, basing the vassal's obedience on the gracious past actions of the great king. Deuteronomy signals the shift from these past actions to the present law in Deuteronomy 4:1 with the words "and now," which transitions the reader from the past to the present. The legal section of Deuteronomy is the longest part of the book (Deut. 4–26). The Ten Commandments are given in Deuteronomy 5, and case laws follow in the next chapters. The case laws are applications of the general principles of the Ten Commandments to specific situations related to the cultural and redemptive-historical moment of Israel (e.g., see chaps. 52 and 101).
4. *Blessings and curses*. From the stipulations flow the treaty's blessings and curses. If the vassal obeys the laws of the treaty, then blessings or rewards will be bestowed on

him and his nation. But if the vassal disobeys the treaty, then curses or punishments will result. Deuteronomy 27–28 lists the blessings and curses of the treaty that depend on whether Israel obeys God's law.

5. *Witnesses*. As a legal agreement between two parties, a treaty has witnesses to its terms. Ancient Near Eastern treaties usually contain long lists of witnesses, typically the gods and goddesses of both countries. Although Deuteronomy is a sermon and not a treaty, Moses does cite witnesses when he calls Israel to respond:

> Today I have given you the choice between life and death, between blessings and curses. Now I call on heaven and earth to witness the choice you make. Oh, that you would choose life, so that you and your descendants might live! You can make this choice by loving the LORD your God, obeying him, and committing yourself firmly to him. This is the key to your life. And if you love and obey the LORD, you will live long in the land the LORD swore to give your ancestors Abraham, Isaac, and Jacob. (Deut. 30:19–20)

The book of Deuteronomy reflects the structure and contents of a treaty between a great king and a vassal people. God is the great king, and Israel is his vassal people. Here in Deuteronomy, Israel the vassal reaffirms its relationship to God, their sovereign king, before they enter the promised land.

The comparison between Deuteronomy and an ancient Near Eastern treaty gives us a deeper understanding of the nature of a covenant, the typical English word used to describe the relationship between God and Israel. *Covenant* is a legal term that describes a relationship between two parties, and a treaty is a particular type of agreement. This covenant/treaty honors God as Israel's king and acknowledges that Israel is his vassal people.

86. "You must not have any other god but me"

» Deut. 5:7

The first commandment calls for the exclusive worship of Yahweh, the god of Israel. It follows from the preamble in the previous verse where God reminds the Israelites that he was the one "who rescued you from the land of Egypt, the place of your slavery" (Deut. 5:6). Notice that the commandments come after this declaration that God rescued them from Egypt. In other words, God's rescue of Israel precedes the obligation of law. Grace precedes law. God does not say that his people needed to obey him in order to earn their salvation from Egypt. No, he rescues them and then tells them through the law how they must respond in obedience to him.

The first four commandments concern the relationship between God and his people; the final six regulate relationships between people. Thus, the first commandment is foundational for the relationship between God and his people. They are not to have any other god except Yahweh.

Notice this commandment does not insist there are no other gods. Even if there are other gods, the people must worship only Yahweh. This lesson is important, because there are other gods that compete for the attention of God's people. Earlier we looked at Exodus 12:12 where God announced on the eve of the final plague that he would have victory that night over the gods of Egypt (chap. 46). The assumption was that these gods were real. These gods were not equals of Yahweh; indeed, they were created by Yahweh. They were demonic forces.

The point is that sometimes the Old Testament uses the Hebrew word we translate "god" or "God" (*'elohim*) to refer to other spiritual powers and authorities, both bad (like the Egyptian gods) and good. The good *'elohim* are more often called angels. Later, we will look at an example in Deuteronomy 32:8 (chap. 108).

The first commandment is clear. Whether or not there are other gods, the only one who deserves worship is Yahweh.

Worshiping any other god, whether a real spiritual force or a figment of imagination, violates the most important and foundational commandment.

87. "You must not make for yourself an idol of any kind"

» Deut. 5:8; 5:8–10

The second commandment prohibits constructing images of any god—whether a false god or even of Yahweh himself—for the purpose of worship. The commandment is straightforward, but its rationale might not be obvious.

First, this prohibition is unique in the ancient Near Eastern world. All of Israel's neighbors—the Egyptians, Mesopotamians, Canaanites, and more—made idols of their gods and directed their worship toward them. Isaiah will later ridicule this worship as he describes how a craftsperson takes a piece of wood and chops it in half. With half the wood he builds a fire to warm himself, and with the other half he makes an idol of his god and bows down to worship it (Isa. 44:6–20). Ancient Near Eastern people did not actually think the idol was the god itself; they thought their god took up residence in the idol. The Mesopotamians would perform an "opening of the eyes and mouth" ritual that would enliven the idol before they directed worship of their god toward it. They also fed, dressed, and washed the idol. They would even parade it in public to attract the people's worship.

Second, the rationale for Israel not to make an idol even of Yahweh was that the creator should not be confused with the creation. God created everything; thus he could not be worshiped in the form of a created thing. He told the people, "You must not make for yourself an idol of any kind, or an image of anything in heaven or on the earth or in the sea" (Deut. 5:8). To worship God in the form of an image was to offend God and his nature as a spiritual being.

Worshiping an image also violated the status of humans as God's image. According to Genesis 1:27, "God created human beings in his own image." To be created in God's image was analogous to a king setting up a statue of himself in order to represent his power and authority in his kingdom (see chap. 4). Human image bearers are not God, and they are not the object of worship, but they are his agents in his creation. They reflect God's glory like the moon reflects the light of the sun. For humans to create an image of God not only violates the nature of God but also the status of humans.

88. "You must not misuse the name of the LORD your God"

» Deut. 5:11

The third commandment prohibits the misuse of God's name, and its deliberate vagueness illustrates an interesting feature of many of the commandments. The commandment begs the question, How does one misuse God's name? The commandment itself does not tell us. The case laws that follow the Ten Commandments give examples of how some commandments are violated in a specific way, but in the final analysis, we have to use our common sense to determine what a misuse might be. One reason the commandment does not specify how one misuses God's name is because there are many ways in which it might be misused.

Some are obvious. To seal a promise by calling on God's name when one is lying would misuse his name. To use it in a vile curse would be misuse. We could go on with the obvious; anything that dishonors God's name, besmirching his reputation and therefore his character, surely would violate this commandment.

But there are also less obvious ways to misuse God's name, including using it flippantly or superficially. A contemporary example would be saying "OMG" to express surprise. This does not bring honor to God's name.

This commandment can also be violated by not using God's name to glorify, praise, or worship God. Conservative Jewish men and women seek to obey this commandment by never speaking the name of God, particularly the name he gave to Moses at the burning bush—Yahweh (Exod. 3:13–15). They reason that if we never use the name of God at all, we cannot misuse it. This practice is based on the very appropriate sense that God's name is especially holy. Even so, the psalmist often praises God's name and instructs his hearers to do the same (e.g., Pss. 7:17; 9:2; 22:22; 30:4).

What some Bible translations render "misuse the name" can be rendered "must not carry the name in vain." This translation reveals another way in which the third commandment might be violated. Earlier in Exodus, we read that the high priest wore a chestpiece with twelves stones, one for each tribe. In this way the high priest would "carry the names of the tribes of Israel" into the presence of God (Exod. 28:29). The priest represented the tribes by carrying their names. Similarly, the Israelites were to carry God's name as God's representatives in the world. They had a priestly role among the nations (19:6). The commandment demanded that they represent God well in the world; when their words or actions reflected badly on God, they violated the commandment.

89. "You must not covet"

» Deut. 5:21

The Old Testament is often wrongly understood to focus only on outward behavior, not on the heart. The first nine commandments can be understood in that way when read in isolation from the tenth commandment. Worship the one true God. Don't make idols. Don't misuse God's name (or misrepresent him). Observe the Sabbath. Honor your father and mother. Don't murder. Don't commit adultery. Don't steal. Don't lie.

Jesus's words in the Sermon on the Mount seem to reinforce the idea that the Old Testament is only interested in right behavior. Jesus tells his Jewish audience that their ancestors were told not to murder, but he says they sin if they are angry with someone or call them an idiot or curse them (Matt. 5:21–22). Similarly, he said the commandment demands that they not commit adultery, but he says they sin if they lust in their hearts (5:27–30).

However, the tenth commandment—do not covet—undercuts the idea that the Old Testament is only interested in externals. To covet something is to deeply desire it. The tenth commandment internalizes all the other commandments. The commandment itself says, "You must not covet your neighbor's wife," which prohibits lust. It goes on to prohibit coveting "your neighbor's house or land, male or female servant, ox or donkey, or anything else that belongs to your neighbor." In other words, if a person yearns to possess something that belongs to someone else, they don't have to steal it to violate God's will. Though not explicitly stated, the logic of the commandments would prohibit hating someone to the point of desiring to harm them, so God's commandments prohibit hate that leads to murder as well as murder itself.

But why does Jesus say "you have heard" do not murder or commit adultery and then say that he prohibits hate and lust? Many wrongly hear Jesus say, "You have heard it said in the Old Testament," but we have seen that the Old Testament already teaches these things. Jesus is not saying "you have heard it said" in the Old Testament, but rather "you have heard your teachers say." He is not correcting the Old Testament; rather, he is correcting the teachers of his own day.

90. "Show them no mercy"

» Deut. 7:2

Here is the first of two places in Deuteronomy where God commands the destruction of the Canaanites who lived in the promised land (see also chap. 98; Deut. 20). Moses is preaching to those Israelites who are about to enter the land and who will encounter the populations that live there. They are "greater and more numerous" than the Israelites, but Moses tells the people to "completely destroy them." Indeed, they must "show them no mercy" (7:1–2; for more on "complete destruction" [*herem*], see Longman, *Confronting Old Testament Controversies*, 123–206).

Today, such a command strikes many readers as heartless, even barbaric. Some try to explain away the picture of God as a warrior who commands his people to wage war. They sometimes pit the God of the Old Testament against the New Testament picture of God in Jesus. The Old Testament God, they say, is a God of wrath and judgment, but in the New Testament, God is merciful and loving.

However, this perspective does not take seriously either the Old or New Testament depiction of God. The Bible as a whole presents a unified and coherent picture of God who fights against human and spiritual evil. That said, God's battle takes on different complexions in the Old and New Testaments but comes together in the picture of the final judgment in the New Testament.

Deuteronomy 7 and 20 both speak to God's battle against Israel's flesh-and-blood enemies, like the Canaanites. These chapters prepare us for the story of the conquest in the book of Joshua and battles like the one at Jericho, where God fights for Israel and causes the Canaanite city to fall (Josh. 6). But God does not fight for Israel all the time; he also fights against Israel if they do not repent of their sin. Examples include the battle of Ai that follows the battle at Jericho (7:1–8:29), the Philistines' defeat of Israel and capture of the ark at the time of the judge Eli (1 Sam. 4:1–11), and most dramatically, the Babylonian defeat of Jerusalem (Lam. 2).

The Old Testament ends with God's people under the thumb of a foreign power. After the Babylonians come the Persians, and after the Persians come the Greeks. By the time of the New Testament, the Romans are in control. The exilic and postexilic prophets like Daniel, Zechariah, and Malachi look into the future and see the coming of God the warrior to save them (Dan. 7; Zech. 14; Mal. 4).

The New Testament opens with the same expectation, as John the Baptist announces that one is coming after him who will chop down unproductive trees and burn chaff with "never-ending fire" (Matt. 3:12). John baptizes Jesus, but rather than chopping and burning, Jesus goes out and heals the sick, gives sight to the blind, preaches the good news to the poor, and more (11:5).

As the story continues, Jesus intensifies and heightens the battle so that it is directed toward the evil spiritual powers and authorities. These enemies are defeated by Jesus's death, not by killing. That is why Christ's work on the cross is sometimes described using military language (e.g., Eph. 4:8; Col. 1:13–15).

But John the Baptist was not wrong. He just did not understand that Christ was coming twice—the second time to complete the victory over the forces of human and spiritual evil. Among other places in the New Testament, the book of Revelation describes this final judgment and brings the account of God's victory over evil to a conclusion (see especially Rev. 19:11–21).

God's warring activity, whether he engages directly or uses human agents like the Israelites, is always connected to his judgment against evil. God is merciful, but he is also a judge who brings justice.

91. "The designated place of worship, the place the LORD your God chooses for his name to be honored"

» Deut. 12:11; 12:1–32

Deuteronomy 12 looks forward to the time when Israel will "drive out the nations that live" in the land of Canaan, the promised land (Deut. 12:2). The setting of Deuteronomy is the plains of Moab, just across from the promised land on the eastern side of the Jordan River. Moses is delivering his final sermon to the generation of Israelites who will enter the land under the leadership of Joshua. Moses himself will ascend Mount Nebo in the Transjordan and die there. His sermon leads the people to reaffirm the covenant with God that their forefathers made at Mount Sinai forty years earlier (see Exod. 19–24). Deuteronomy 12 speaks to God's desire concerning the place they will worship him with sacrifices once they are completely established in the land.

The instruction of Deuteronomy 12 is often called the law of centralization because it calls for one central place of worship, "the place of worship [God] himself will choose from among all the tribes" (Deut. 12:5). This choosing will take place once "he gives you rest from all your enemies and you're living safely in the land" (12:10). Once God chooses that place, it will be the only place where sacrifices may be offered to the Lord.

That future situation stands in contrast to Israel's reality to this point in which they may worship in different places. In the wilderness the main location of sacrifice for the Israelites is the tabernacle, a mobile center for worship (see chap. 61). But they may also build altars at other locations. Not so in the future once there is peace in the land and God chooses this permanent location.

But when did God choose the place? It wouldn't be for many years, even centuries, later. Joshua and the Israelites defeat many Canaanite kings and cities, but even at the time of Joshua's death, there are still large parts of the promised land controlled by the Canaanites.

Indeed, God does not make clear his choice of the place until the time of David. David was the one who completed the conquest, subduing the enemies within the land, but he was not the one to build the divinely chosen worship center, the temple (see 1 Chron. 28:3). In fact, when David announced he would build the temple, God said no (2 Sam. 7:1–11).

At the same time, God told David his son would build the temple at the place that God would choose—namely, Mount Zion in Jerusalem. It was appropriate for Solomon to build the temple and replace the tabernacle, thus representing Israel's establishment in the land, because he would inherit a peaceful kingdom. Indeed, his very name, *Shelomo* in Hebrew, means "peace." And after Solomon built the temple, that was the only place where the Israelites could legitimately offer their sacrifices.

92. "The false prophets . . . must be put to death"

» Deut. 13:5

See chapter 96.

93. "You must not eat any detestable animals that are ceremonially unclean"

» Deut. 14:3; 14:1–21

See chapter 71.

94. "In the seventh year you must set that servant free"

» Deut. 15:12; 15:12–18

See chapter 52.

95. "Be sure to select as king the man the LORD your God chooses"

» Deut. 17:15; 17:14–20

Moses preaches what we know as the book of Deuteronomy on the plains of Moab after forty years of wilderness wandering. He delivers his sermon on the eve of Israel entering the promised land under Joshua's leadership. Up to this moment, Israel had no king and would not have its first king for centuries until Saul is crowned (see 1 Sam. 8–12). Still, at the time of Moses, God gives Israel instructions for choosing a future king.

When God did give Israel its first king, he did so at a time when the people lacked trust in the prophet Samuel and, more importantly, in God himself. The conditions under which Saul became king raise the question of whether kingship was an afterthought, something second-best for Israel. But Deuteronomy 17:14–20 shows that kingship was always the divine intention, and it is not the first place in the Torah that anticipates kingship, as we saw in Genesis 17 (chap. 24), Genesis 49 (chap. 39), and Numbers 24:17 (chap. 85).

Deuteronomy 17:14–20 is a particularly important text because it sets the standard by which the later kings of Israel and Judah will be evaluated in the books of Samuel and Kings. So what kind of king does this passage envision?

The passage imagines the people saying, "We should select a king to rule over us like the other nations around us" (Deut. 17:14; see 1 Sam. 8:5). But the kings of the nations around Israel at that time and into the future were despots who took advantage of their citizens as they did their best to hold on to power. The king that God describes here is quite different from the typical ancient Near Eastern king.

The description begins by saying what a king should not be like. First, he must not be a foreigner but a native Israelite. Second, the king should not be interested in amassing tremendous wealth or power. He should not be interested in personal silver and gold. He must not accumulate "a large stable of horses for himself" (Deut. 17:16), nor must he accumulate wives and build a large harem. Those are negative characteristics that God did not want in a future king. But there is a positive side that is equally crucial.

The king was to be godly and knowledgeable in the law ("he must copy for himself this body of instruction on a scroll," Deut. 17:18). He was to do this in the presence of the Levitical priests, who would have been responsible for the maintenance and transmission of the instruction. The point is that the king must fear God; he must know his place before God. Kings would be tempted to think of themselves as the center of the universe, but through fear they acknowledge God's supremacy and the need to obey him. This would "ensure that he and his descendants will reign for many generations in Israel" (17:20).

The later books of Samuel and Kings that use this law to judge the kings of Israel and Judah will describe how only a few kings met this standard (David, Hezekiah, Josiah), and they did so imperfectly. This law helps explain why the reigns of both the kings of Israel and the kings of Judah would eventually come to an end.

96. "How will we know whether or not a prophecy is from the LORD?"

» Deut. 18:21; 18:15–22

Prophets claimed to speak on behalf of God. But how could the Israelites tell the difference between an authentic spokesperson for God and a false one? The instructions in Deuteronomy 13:1–5 and 18:15–22 provide the answer; they form a pair, describing different conditions that must be present for a prophet to be considered true.

The first instruction informs the reader that even if "the signs or miracles" that the prophet announces take place, the prophet is false if they speak the prophecy in the name of another god and try to get people to follow a false god (Deut. 13:1–3). We observed a good example in Exodus (see chap. 46), where the Egyptian magicians successfully called on their gods to mimic two of the early signs that Moses and Aaron performed. They turned their walking staffs into snakes, and they turned water into blood (Exod. 7:8–24). Even though they were able to perform these signs, they were still false prophets because they represented other gods.

However, some false prophets claimed to represent the true God and speak in his name. Deuteronomy 18 considers this situation. The passage first reminds the people that they asked God to provide a prophet to speak God's word to them. God said he would, and the people should listen to prophets as if God himself were speaking. But if a prophet claimed to speak for God and what that prophet said would happen did *not* happen, then that prophet was a false prophet. This makes sense because God's word is true. If God says something will happen, then it will happen.

However, these instructions concerning prophets raise two issues. First, what if the prophet is speaking about the distant future? For example, in 1 Kings 13 an unnamed prophet declares that the unauthorized altar King Jeroboam built will be desecrated in the time of King Josiah. Jeroboam ruled during the 900s BC, and Josiah was on the throne three hundred years later, during the 600s BC. In this case, there were accompanying signs that took place immediately at the time of Jeroboam. First, a crack appeared in the altar, and when Jeroboam pointed at the prophet, Jeroboam's "hand became paralyzed in that position, and he couldn't pull it back" (1 Kings 13:4). This should have convinced Jeroboam that the prophet's message was from God, but "even after this, Jeroboam did not turn from his evil ways" (13:33).

The second issue concerns when a true prophet does speak in the name of the Lord but the prophecy does not come true. Perhaps the best-known example is Jonah. God told him to tell Nineveh they would be judged because of their sin, but the judgment did not happen as said. Jonah told them, "Forty days from now Nineveh will be destroyed," but forty days later, nothing of the sort happened (Jon. 3:4). Here, however, we know why. The people of Nineveh repented. Prophetic messages of judgment typically, if not always, came with the proviso "unless you repent." And in this case, Nineveh repented.

97. "Eye for eye"

» Deut. 19:21

See chapter 56.

98. "When you go out to fight your enemies"

» Deut. 20:1; 20:1–20

In chapter 90, we considered Deuteronomy 7, the first of two passages in the book with God's instructions about waging war. There I situated Old Testament warfare within the biblical theme of God's battle against evil that starts in Genesis and runs through the end of the book of Revelation. Deuteronomy 20 overlaps with Deuteronomy 7 and further delineates God's will on the matter.

Deuteronomy 20 encourages Israel not to be afraid when they go to war, even when an enemy has superior forces. The reason they should not be afraid is that "the LORD your God, who brought you out of the land of Egypt, is with you!" (20:1). Indeed, Israelite commanders should encourage people who are afraid of the upcoming battle to go home. Rather than exhorting all Israelites to fight, the passage identifies groups who are exempt and should refrain from the fight. These include people who have just built a house but not yet dedicated it, people who have planted a vineyard but not yet enjoyed the produce, and people who are engaged but not yet married.

The reason for the rather cavalier attitude toward numbers of troops is explained by the opening statement in Deuteronomy 20 that God is "with you" in battle. As later battles would illustrate, Israel must go into battle in an inferior position because otherwise they will lose sight of the fact that victory is because of God, not their own strength.

Gideon's battle against the Midianites and their allies in the book of Judges is a prime example of this approach to war in the Old Testament. Thirty-two thousand troops show up for the battle, but God does not want Israel to go into battle at such strength, because when they win, "the Israelites will boast to me that they saved themselves by their own strength" (Judg. 7:2). Even after twenty-two thousand who are afraid are told to go home, God says there are still way too many people. He tells Gideon to take the remaining ten thousand down to the spring to drink. Three hundred men drink the water by cupping it in their hands and lapping it up with their tongues like dogs, while the others put their mouths directly in the stream. The three hundred are the ones chosen to enter the battle, which they win, bringing praise to God. Their method of drinking water does not mark them as special in any way. It was just God's way of getting the army down to its proper size.

The most difficult feature of the instructions in Deuteronomy 20 is the command to "completely destroy the Hittites, Amorites, Canaanites, Perizzites, Hivites, and Jebusites, just as the LORD your God has commanded you" (Deut. 20:17). This issue has been addressed previously (chap. 90), but Deuteronomy 20 differentiates between treatment of enemies inside and enemies outside the promised land (20:10–16). This is because God had determined to judge the people within the land (see chap. 21). The passage also indicates that part of the motivation for destruction was to prevent the Israelites from emulating the false worship of the people who lived in the land (20:18).

The final paragraph of the passage (Deut. 20:19–20) sounds environmentally sensitive. God warns the Israelites not to cut down trees, at least the fruit trees, in the process of war. This command, however, is in the interest of the Israelites themselves. Fruit trees are a food source and would belong to the Israelites once they take over the land. Other trees may be cut down to "make the equipment you need to attack the enemy town until it falls" (20:20).

99. "Suppose you see among the captives a beautiful woman"

» Deut. 21:11; 21:10–14

This passage presents significant ethical issues for a modern reader. The law envisions a soldier who in the context of a battle sees a woman to whom he is attracted and wants to marry. This woman would be a foreigner from outside the land since an earlier passage prohibited the survival of women as well as the men who lived in the land (Deut. 20:16). In such a case, the man must give the woman a month to mourn her family. At the start, she should "shave her head, cut her nails, and change the clothes she was wearing when she was captured" (21:12–13). These actions likely signified a transition from her former life to her present one.

To modern readers, taking a woman in the context of war seems harsh because it robs her of agency. Indeed, many case laws do not legislate God's ideal but take the people where they are and move them toward that ideal. In God's ideal world, there would be no war and no taking of women in this manner. But God's created order has been violated by sin, and the case law actually restrains that sin. The law provides important boundaries and even protections for captured women that were not practiced by Israel's neighbors. Other ancient Near Eastern armies did not restrain, and perhaps even encouraged, war rape and other atrocities.

The law concerns a man who finds himself attracted to a woman captive after a battle. In the ancient Near East (and far too often in warfare today), the soldier would rape the woman, and if he wanted to marry her would simply force her to do so without regard for the trauma she experienced with the loss of her family. In Israel's case, a soldier could take a captured woman in marriage, but he must allow her a month to mourn her parents (the customary length of mourning for an Israelite, Deut. 34:8). There would also be an acknowledgment of her transition by shaving her head, cutting her nails, and giving her a change of clothes.

After a month, however, he may marry her and presumably force her to marry him. In the ancient Near East, if the man changed his mind, he could just force the woman to go away. The Israelite man could do that as well, but there is a proviso that he "may not sell her or treat her as a slave" (Deut. 21:14). This restriction carries a potentially disturbing rationale. He is not allowed to sell or enslave her because he has "humiliated her" (Deut. 21:14), a statement that is ambiguous to modern interpreters. The word here is the same Hebrew word (*'anah*) used in the account of Jacob's daughter Dinah, though sometimes the word is translated using different English words in Genesis 34:2 and Deuteronomy 21:14, even within the same Bible translation.

The situation in Genesis 34 has similarities to the one addressed by the law in Deuteronomy, though it is not in the context of battle. The prince of the Canaanite city of Shechem sees Jacob's daughter and "humiliates" (ESV) her, which almost certainly means he rapes her (NLT, NIV). He then wants to marry her. Because of the similar wording and situation, the soldier's "humiliation" of the woman in Deuteronomy 21:14 could mean that he raped her on the battlefield before he married her. While this is a possible understanding or maybe even a probable one, the word could refer to a different type of humiliation, like the very act of casting her aside after marrying her. In either case, as hard as the first possibility is to us as modern readers, the biblical law is still an improvement on the typical practice of the time and place. Remember, in Old Testament case law God often takes the people where they are and moves them toward his ideal. That progression would go further in the New Testament and beyond. Certainly today this law should never be used to justify war rape or compulsory marriage.

100. "This son of ours is stubborn and rebellious and refuses to obey"

» Deut. 21:20; 21:18–21

This law is one of several concerning difficult children. Exodus 21:15 calls for the death penalty for children who strike or attack their parents. Exodus 21:17 does the same for those who curse or dishonor their parents (see also Deut. 27:16). Deuteronomy 21:18–21 is the most detailed of the laws and is the focus of this chapter, but the discussion will shed light on the other passages as well.

As noted, case laws apply general principles of the Ten Commandments to specific situations. All the case laws concerning difficult children go back to the fifth commandment: "Honor your father and mother, as the Lord your God commanded you. Then you will live a long, full life in the land the Lord your God is giving you" (Deut. 5:16; see also Exod. 20:12). All these laws illustrate different ways in which children do not honor their parents.

Still, the laws seem harsh, particularly if they apply to young children who may occasionally act in ways that anger their parents. But it is wrong to envision the law in this way, and it ignores some of the safeguards that are built in.

First, we are not to think of the "son" here as a young boy. This is evident in the description of him as "a glutton and a drunkard" (Deut. 21:20); young children's consumption would be monitored and controlled by parents. We shouldn't think of the parents hauling their preadolescent children to court.

Second, we are not to think that the judgment is based on occasional acts. The description of the son indicates a deeply twisted character. He is "stubborn and rebellious" (Deut. 21:18) as well as a glutton and a drunkard.

Third, the parents initiate the investigation. Nearly all parents would be extremely reluctant to make such a serious charge unless the behavior was dangerous. If anything, parents would err on the side of not reporting the bad character of their children.

Fourth, the parents don't make the final call; the elders in a court do, which implies an investigation. While most parents would be reluctant to report a troubled child, some parents are twisted themselves and might do so for a variety of reasons. Indeed, in an ancient society where the father was the ultimate decision maker, the requirement to take the child to court provided a measure of protection against an angry father who might kill a son in a moment of rage.

Fifth, the death penalty was almost certainly not the only remedy for the crime, but the maximum penalty in really bad cases (see chap. 57). Other lesser penalties might usually be applied.

Finally, the law probably functioned more as a warning to grown children and their parents. It clearly communicated to children the negative consequences that could come if they did not heed their parents' warnings, and it communicated to parents the importance of instructing and disciplining their children.

On the surface, this law and ones like it strike us as harsh, almost barbaric. But when read carefully and in context, they actually protect families who might have a dangerous grown child, and they protect children who might be prey to the whims of off-balanced parents.

101. "You must build a railing around the edge of its flat roof"

» Deut. 22:8

This law sounds strange to modern readers, especially those in the American suburbs. It requires a new home builder to put a railing, or fence, around the edge of the roof of the house. The Hebrew simply says "roof," not "flat roof," but the NLT appropriately translates with "flat" because ancient Israelite houses had flat roofs, a feature that is relevant to understanding the law.

Case laws apply the Ten Commandments to specific situations relevant for the cultural and redemptive-historical period of the time, and this law applies the sixth commandment, "You must not murder" (Deut. 5:17; see Exod. 20:13). This commandment not only prohibits the active illegitimate killing of a person, but it also requires that people take steps to protect the safety of others. Roofs of houses in ancient Israel were also used for living space, so it was important to make sure that no one fell off and hurt or even killed themselves.

This law illustrates why the case laws in general should not be automatically and literally applied today without reflecting on whether our cultural and redemptive-historical moment has changed from circumstances that made the law relevant. For those whose roofs are not flat and/or are not used for living space, it would be ridiculous to require the building of a railing.

On the other hand, readers today can still learn from this law. How would the sixth commandment apply to the construction of houses today? To answer this question, we have to think through potential and especially common hazards in our particular houses. Does the house have a swimming pool into which people, particularly children, might fall and drown? A fence would be required in that case. Electrical sockets in the presence of children? Then plastic covers for those not in use. That is the type of reasoning this law encourages.

102. "You must not wear clothing made of wool and linen woven together"

» Deut. 22:11; 22:9–11

See chapter 75.

103. "But never give more than forty lashes"

» Deut. 25:3; 25:1–3

This law speaks generally of a dispute that is taken to a court overseen by a judge. The judge is to acquit the innocent and sentence the guilty. The passage goes on to consider cases in which the judge sentences the guilty person to be flogged. While flogging is still practiced in parts of the world and was practiced in America for much of its history, many of today's readers find the idea unsettling at best.

Given that the Old Testament law takes people where they are and moves them toward God's ideal, we need to consider Israel's context. In the surrounding culture, an Assyrian law code allowed fifty lashes for a crime. The Babylonian Code of Hammurabi permitted sixty, and Egyptian laws allowed for a hundred and even two hundred lashes. Deuteronomy mandates no more than forty. The number of lashes were to be "appropriate to the crime" (Deut. 25:2). Since forty was the maximum, it would only be applied in the most egregious circumstances.

Interestingly, the reason for the limit is not physical but psychological. The reason a judge could not permit more than forty lashes is because it "would publicly humiliate your neighbor" (Deut. 25:3). Furthermore, it is surprising that the criminal is described as a "neighbor." In the ancient context of this passage, the prohibition of more than forty lashes is considered humane.

104. "Her husband's brother should marry her and have intercourse with her to fulfill the duties of a brother-in-law"

» Deut. 25:5: 25:5–10

This law details what should happen if a married man dies and leaves no sons behind. The deceased's brother was to marry his widow so she could have a child (or children). In this way, the brother would "fulfill the duties of a brother-in-law" (Deut. 25:5). The first son born of this union would be considered the son of the deceased man.

The purpose of this law was to protect a family line and inheritance rights. The son would inherit his father's property. Another social consequence was the well-being of the woman.

In an ancient Near Eastern society, a woman not protected by a husband or a son was vulnerable. This law protected her.

The law then considers what happens if the brother refuses to fulfill his obligation. After all, marrying the widow would work against the man's own self-interest since if the deceased brother has no heir then the surviving brother inherits his property (Num. 27:8–11). In such a case, the woman goes to the elders and tells them of his refusal. They confront the man, and if he continues to refuse, then the woman pulls off his sandal and spits in his face, an act of contempt in ancient as well as modern society. He not only shames himself but his family who will be called "the family of the man whose sandal was pulled off" (Deut. 25:10).

This law helps explain two stories in the Old Testament, one before Moses and one after. The first concerns Judah, one of Jacob's twelve sons, and is in Genesis 38 (see chap. 35). The second story is in the book of Ruth, where the Moabite Ruth was married to an Israelite man. This man was the son of a woman named Naomi whose family had left their home in Bethlehem to go to Moab to survive a famine. When all the men in the family die, Naomi returns to Bethlehem with Ruth accompanying her.

There is no brother-in-law in Bethlehem, but there are relatives, including a landowner named Boaz who treats Ruth well as she gleans in his fields. When Ruth makes it clear that she is interested in marrying him, he says a nearer relative has a prior right to the marriage. Boaz, interested in marrying Ruth, approaches that relative and starts by talking about property. This unnamed man has the right to buy the land of Elimelech, Ruth's deceased husband. He is interested until he hears that if he buys the property he also needs to marry Ruth so "she can have children who will carry on her husband's name and keep the land in the family" (Ruth 4:5). He refuses because it threatens his own estate. At this point, he takes off his sandal and hands it to Boaz. This ritual in Ruth is not described as a statement of contempt but as a transference of the right to purchase the property.

The case law in Deuteronomy 25:5–10 applies the principles of both the seventh (prohibiting adultery) and the eighth (prohibiting theft) commandments according to the social and redemptive-historical moment of the people of God. The law served to keep property in the right family, clan, and tribe.

105. "You must destroy the Amalekites and erase their memory from under heaven"

» Deut. 25:19; 25:17–19

Earlier in Deuteronomy, God instructed Israel to completely destroy the people in the land, "the Hittites, Girgashites, Amorites, Canaanites, Perizzites, Hivites, and Jebusites" (Deut. 7:1–6; see chap. 90). This command was not to make room for the Israelites to live in the land promised to them, though it accomplished that over time. The main reason for God's command is that these people's sin deserved judgment and Israel was God's instrument of judgment, just as the Babylonians will be God's instrument of judgment on sinful Judah (Hab. 1:2–12). Though God did not allow Israel to present "terms of peace" to those in the land, they could to those who lived in "distant towns" (Deut. 20:10–15). The Amalekites were a nomadic tribe or confederation of tribes who were not listed among the people who lived in the land. At various times, they inhabited a part of the promised land, but they don't seem to be part of the settled inhabitants. So, why were they singled out in this law for destruction?

The law recalls the reason as it reminds Israel to never "forget what the Amalekites did to you as you came from Egypt. They attacked you when you were exhausted and weary, and they struck down those who were straggling behind" (Deut. 25:17–18). The reference is to the conflict at Rephidim, a location on the Sinai Peninsula where Israel camped not long after leaving Egypt (Exod. 17:8–16). The law highlights the devious nature of the Amalekites' attack, picking off stragglers. Joshua led the counterattack, and as long as Moses held his walking staff, symbolizing God's presence, above his head, Israel had the upper hand and eventually won the battle. Moses then told the people that the Amalekites had "raised their fist against the LORD's throne, so now the LORD will be at war with Amalek generation after generation" (Exod. 17:16). Deuteronomy says the Amalekites did what they did because "they had no fear of God" (Deut. 25:17).

Amalek continued to cause trouble for Israel after the events at Rephidim. When Moses sent the twelve spies into the promised land, they encountered Amalekites in the Negev. Ten of the spies then persuade Israel that they cannot successfully enter the land. God is angry with these spies and with the people, telling them they will spend forty years in the wilderness. In response, the people foolishly try to enter the land anyway, but the Amalekites defeat them (Num. 13–14). Later, during the period of the judges, some Amalekites would align themselves with various oppressors of Israel (Judg. 3:13; 6:33; 7:12).

It is not until the time of Saul that Israel has an opportunity to follow through on Deuteronomy's instruction to destroy the Amalekites. Saul defeats them but not completely, bringing Samuel's (and God's) anger down on them (1 Sam. 15; 28:18). This failure costs Saul the kingship, which will be given "to someone else" (15:28).

That someone else is David. Before he became king, he was living among the Philistines (to hide from Saul). He and his personal army raided the Amalekites, among others who are described as living "toward the land of Egypt" (1 Sam. 27:8). Later, while David and his men were away, the Amalekites destroyed their home base in Ziklag. David and his men pursued them and destroyed them "except 400 young men who fled on camels" (30:17).

The order to destroy the Amalekites is finally fulfilled at the very end of the Old Testament story as recounted in the book of Esther. The Persian king Xerxes decides to eradicate the Jewish community in his empire on the advice of Haman, who is described as an Agagite, reminiscent of the king of Amalek at the time of Saul, Agag (Esther 3:1; 1 Sam. 15:8). Mordecai, Esther's cousin, is said to be "from the tribe of Benjamin and . . . a descendant of Kish and Shimei" (Esther 2:5), which relates him to Saul (1 Sam. 9:1; 2 Sam. 16:5). Thus, the book of Esther presents a replay of the conflict between Saul and the Amalekites but here with the result that the Agagite Haman is destroyed by the descendants of Kish.

106. "Cursed is anyone who dishonors father or mother"

» Deut. 27:16

See chapter 100.

107. "You will eat the flesh of your own sons and daughters"

» Deut. 28:53; 28:53–57

The essay introducing the book of Deuteronomy described the relationship between Deuteronomy and the form of an ancient Near Eastern vassal treaty. The analogy between the two demonstrates that the biblical concept of a covenant is more closely identified as a treaty. In such a treaty, gracious past actions of a sovereign toward a vassal obligate that vassal to obey the laws set by the sovereign. In Deuteronomy the legal section is the longest part of the book (4:1–26:19). After the law come blessings and curses—blessings for obedience and curses for disobedience to the law. Indeed, the section of curses begins, "But if you refuse to listen to the Lord your God and do not obey all the commands and decrees I am giving you today, all these curses will come and overwhelm you" (28:15).

The curse in Deuteronomy 28:53–57 (with a parallel in Lev. 26:29) is illustrative of the other curses that follow. These curses speak of God sending disease and drought but especially military defeat, destruction, and exile. Deuteronomy 28:53 describes the consequences of an enemy's siege against the covenant/treaty breakers. A prolonged siege was a chief military strategy to bring a walled city like Jerusalem to its knees, sparing the need to breach the walls. The food for walled cities came from outside the wall, and a siege prevented provisions into the city. The intent was to starve a city into submission. Deuteronomy's curse imagines the extremes of a siege where parents would eat their own children. The curse warns that desperation will reduce even the most refined people to barbarity.

For Deuteronomy, war and its horrors are not simply natural outcomes of violating God's law. Rather they are the direct intervention of God (see 28:20, 22, 24–25, 27–28, 35–37, 48–49, 59–61, 63–65, 68, which all name the Lord as the agent of the suffering). Still, it is the people who will bear the ultimate responsibility for what happens to them because it is their disobedience that triggers the curses.

These curses are warnings. Along with the covenant blessings (Deut. 28:1–14), they intend to encourage the people to maintain their proper relationship with God. Unfortunately, as time goes on, God's people do not heed the warnings to live according to the laws God gave them for their flourishing.

In response to his people's rebellion, God sent prophets to warn the people that if they did not repent, then the covenant curses would come upon them. For example, before the Babylonian siege of Jerusalem, Jeremiah warned the unrepentant people that God would "see to it that your enemies lay siege to the city until all the food is gone. Then those trapped inside will eat their own sons and daughters and friends. They will be driven to utter despair" (Jer. 19:9; see also Ezek. 5:10).

But the people did not listen, so the curses came on them in the form of the Babylonian destruction of Jerusalem in 586 BC and the resultant exile. The book of Lamentations looks back on the destruction and grieves that "tenderhearted women have cooked their own children. They have eaten them to survive the siege" (Lam. 4:10).

The curses of the covenant are hard to read. Many describe brutal consequences of not obeying God. However, God does not make parents eat their children in a siege. Rather, he warns them that violating his law has consequences, and he will use their enemies to punish them; when that happens, some out of desperation will engage in acts that they cannot imagine.

108. "He fixed the boundaries of the peoples according to the number of the gods"

» Deut. 32:8 (NRSVue); 32:7–9

Moses, at the end of his life and before the people enter the land, recites a song in front of the entire assembly. He has just led the people to reaffirm their covenant with God (see the essay introducing this section, "The Book of Deuteronomy"). Now he recites to them a song, which includes the difficult text of Deuteronomy 32:8.

Moses begins by invoking the heavens and the earth to hear his song, perhaps because they were earlier cited as witnesses to the covenant made between Israel and God (Deut. 30:19). Indeed, God wanted Moses to write this song to function as a witness against Israel when they later break the covenant (31:16–19).

The song then praises God as a "faithful God who does no wrong," in contrast to his "corrupt" children who are a "deceitful and twisted generation" (Deut. 32:4–5). The next section and the stanzas that follow look back on God's goodness to his people (32:7–14). Then the song turns to how the people he had made prosperous turned against him and "offered sacrifices to demons, which are not God, to gods they had not known before" (32:17). In response to their infidelity, God will reject them and make them suffer (32:19–35). However, eventually "the Lord will give justice to his people, and he will change his mind about his servants" when they see that their gods are false and cannot save them (32:36–38). The song ends with God's declaration that he puts to death and brings to life and "will avenge the blood of his children; he will take revenge against his enemies" (32:43). The song's purpose was to remind the people to obey God. When the people are unfaithful to their God, the song functions as a witness against them.

This summary provides the context for Deuteronomy 32:7–9. The passage is part of the reflection on God's past gracious acts toward his people. The difficult text is specifically in verse 8, a difficulty that can be seen by comparing English translations that reflect different ancient versions of the text. Throughout this book, we have been citing the NLT, which renders this verse "he established the boundaries of the peoples according to the number in his heavenly court." The ESV is similar to the NLT: "according to the number of the sons of God." These renditions are not wrong but are not as clear as the NRSVue translation above. They all differ from the NIV: "he set up boundaries for the peoples according to the number of the sons of Israel." What accounts for the difference between the NIV and the NRSVue/NLT/ESV translations?

We start with the variance in the ancient manuscripts. The NIV follows the Hebrew Masoretic Text, while the NRSVue, NLT, and ESV follow evidence provided by the ancient Greek translation (the Septuagint) and the Dead Sea Scrolls. The Masoretic Text is usually preferred to the Septuagint, except in cases where the Septuagint is supported by the Dead Sea Scrolls, as in this verse. (To be more precise, the Septuagint translated the Hebrew represented in the Dead Sea Scrolls as "the angels of God.")

In terms of deciding which ancient manuscript should be preferred, we consider what is more likely: (1) A later scribe substituted the idea that God distributed the nations to different gods with the idea that he distributed them to the sons of Israel, or (2) the translator of the Septuagint substituted the idea that God distributed the nations to the sons of Israel with the idea that God distributed them to different gods. The first of these is likely, while the second is not. Thus, it is highly likely that the NRSVue/NLT/ESV got it right. But this still leaves us with the question, How do we understand what the text claims?

The text claims that God distributed the nations (implied by "boundaries of the people") to the "sons of God" or "the gods" (or, as in the Septuagint, "the angels of God"). This passage uses the language of what scholars call the divine council. In the literature of Israel's neighbors this refers to the council of the gods, who were ruled over by the chief god. The Old Testament sometimes uses "gods" or "sons of gods" to refer to what we would call angels or demons (see chap. 86). These gods or beings are not equal to God; indeed, God created them.

Daniel 10 provides an example of this distribution of the nations to the sons of God, or the angels. Daniel has been praying and fasting for three weeks, and in response to his prayers an angel comes with a message. The angel explains his three-week delay by saying that the spirit prince of Persia had blocked his way until Michael, identified as "your spirit prince" (10:21), had come to his aid. Later, when the angel speaks of his departure, he says that he will have to fight the spirit prince of Greece. These are spiritual beings, sons of God, who are associated with particular nations.

109. "Your faithful servants the Levites"

» Deut. 33:8; 33:8–11

See chapter 64.

ACKNOWLEDGMENTS

As a longtime teacher of the Bible, I am very aware that many Christians struggle to understand a number of passages in the Old Testament. I went into Old Testament studies decades ago because I had my own questions and also wanted to help others to appreciate the importance of the Old Testament for our theology and life.

It's been my privilege to engage the Old Testament over the years and to teach it and write about it. Many passages continue to be tough texts for me, but even the most difficult teach us something about God, ourselves, and our world. I am happy to share what I know (and what I don't know) about these passages in this book.

This book is the first in what will be a series of four books. This volume covers the Pentateuch, or Torah, the first five books of the Old Testament. The Pentateuch provides the foundation for the rest of the Old Testament and indeed for the whole Christian Bible.

I would like to thank Derek Brown, formerly of Lexham Press, for suggesting that I write this series to complement the work of Murray J. Harris, who wrote the two-volume *Navigating Tough*

Texts: A Guide to Problem Passages in the New Testament. By the time I finished this first volume, Baker Books had acquired Lexham Press and so will publish the series moving forward. Having worked with Baker in their trade and academic divisions for many years, I am very pleased with this development. I want to thank both Brian Vos and Amy Nemecek of Baker Books for their excellent editorial work.

I also want to acknowledge my wife, Alice, whose support and love have made my work possible. This book is dedicated to our two oldest granddaughters, Gabrielle and Mia Longman, daughters of our oldest son, Tremper IV. When this book is published in fall 2026, Gabrielle will be a senior at the University of Southern California and Mia will be a senior at Conard High School in West Hartford, Connecticut. Nanny and I hope you both have a wonderful senior year as you prepare for the next stage of your lives. We love you very much.

WORKS CITED

Augustine. *The Literal Meaning of Genesis*. Translated by John Hammond Taylor. Newman Press, 1982.

Foster, Benjamin R., trans. "Atra-ḫasis." *COS* 1.130:450–53.

Longman, Tremper III. *Confronting Old Testament Controversies: Pressing Questions about Evolution, Sexuality, History, and Violence.* Baker, 2019.

Longman, Tremper III. *The Bible and the Ballot: Using Scripture in Political Decisions.* Eerdmans, 2020.

Origen. *On First Principles* (*De Principiis*). In vol. 4 of *The Ante-Nicene Fathers*. Edited by Alexander Roberts and James Donaldson. 1885–1887. Repr., Hendrickson, 1994.

Pardee, Dennis, trans. "The ʾAqhatu Legend." *COS* 1.103:343–56.

Levine, Baruch A., trans. "The Deir ʿAlla Plaster Inscription." *COS* 2.27: 140–44.

TREMPER LONGMAN III (PhD, Yale University) is Distinguished Scholar and Professor Emeritus of Biblical Studies at Westmont College. Before going to Westmont, he taught at Westminster Theological Seminary in Philadelphia for eighteen years. He has served in leadership for the Institute for Biblical Research for many years. Longman is the author of more than thirty books, including biblical commentaries, scholarly works, and popular books on how to interpret the Bible. He is also a senior translator and a member of the Bible Translation Committee for the New Living Translation. He lives in Alexandria, Virginia.